Really help you

Worst weeds, Companion plants and Co-lives, for farmers and horticulturists

With commercial growing small margins are very important. A few percentages improvement in yield, or a similar decrease in rejects, can make a crop much more profitable. But only when the additional costs to obtain that change at the margin are less than the increase in profit.

As the costs of most inputs continually increase it becomes more economic to employ methods that involve fewer such imports. For any business with land there should be little simpler and lower cost than encouraging certain plants (often on non-cropping land such as verges). If these sustain more predators and parasites that reduce insect damage to the crops then these are well worth employing. Similarly other plants can be included to sustain more pollinators. Likewise a reduction in weed competition is generally repaid with an increase in yields. However it's equally important to know which weeds are most pernicious and thus most in need of control as otherwise effort may be wasted on relatively benign ones.

Contains selected data on farm, orchard and horticultural crops from these three prior volumes;

Volume 1. Plants, their good & bad companions and worst weeds
Volume 2. Plants and Lepidoptera; the caterpillars and thus the butterflies these plants support

Volume 3. Plants & their other co-lives: associated insects, fauna, nematodes, bacteria & fungi large and small

Bob Flowerdew

Contents

Dedication- to all those hard working people of the soil who feed everyone else often unthanked and always under-rewarded!

INTRODUCTION to Really help your crops

With commercial growing small margins are very important. A few percentage improvement in yield, or a similar decrease in rejects, can make a crop more profitable. But only if the additional costs to obtain that change at the margin are less than the increase in profit.

As the costs of most inputs continually increase it becomes more economic to employ methods that involve fewer such imports. For any business with land and someone a grower there should be little simpler and lower cost than encouraging certain plants (often on non-cropping land such as verges) from cuttings or self saved seed. If these sustain more predators and parasites that reduce insect damage to the crops then these are well worth employing. Similarly other plants can be included to sustain more pollinators.

Likewise a reduction in weed competition is generally repaid with an increase in yields. However it's become evident that many weeds do not just compete by abstracting nutrients, air, light or water from our crops but many also compete by adding substances to the environment damaging to our crops. The most costly to our crops are those weeds that add germination and emergence inhibitors to the soil thus reducing the stand of a crop, especially significant as seed costs rise. A serious reduction until now little considered is found from trash hanging over from a previous crop.

And some plants pollen, deliberately or accidentally, reduces the set of seed in others.

It's well known that our native Berberis plants were mostly eradicated when these were discovered to be alternate hosts for a rust disease of wheat. Likewise there are a huge number of other diseases, and pests, of our crops that have alternate hosts of native and garden plants. If it's possible and economic to remove these from the vicinity then the pest or disease incidence is likely to also be reduced. Or if we can increase the number of beneficial insects controlling these by eating them, then the effect is similar.

Viruses are a particularly difficult problem and these also often have alternate or multiple plant hosts many of which associations are seldom considered. Not allowing these hosts to proliferate in the vicinity will prevent some potential outbreaks.

And then there are the more traditional companion effects where some crops just seem to do better mixed with or nearby some and poorer with others. Some of these are acting through changes to the root environment with substances altering the variety and proportions of soil microorganisms. These substances do not necessarily break down quickly and may persist thus altering the performance of a future crop. Rotations other than for the major field crops have seldom been evaluated scientifically if ever and it may greatly alter some crops performance to follow this or that crop and not others. As growers diversify this may be a rich field to investigate.

This book is the distillation of several decades of research into texts ancient and modern noting many different associations and co-lives; here selected for farm and horticultural crops.

I am a gardener, not a specialist, and these are all associations I have come across, a few have been empirically trialled by myself and I note these. However I do not present any of these entries as guaranteed scientific fact but as indications worthy of research.

So here are the traditional good and bad companionships noted since Classical times, the adverse effects of weeds and other plants on the germination and growth of their 'competitors', the caterpillars (and thus the butterflies) that are sustained by these plants, and the huge array of other co-lives big and small, animal and vegetable that each entry supports in the magnificent web of life.

As crops have been under cultivation for some time these have developed a whole 'new' web of interactions over and above those they experienced in an un-crowded and more diverse state of Nature. Rather predictably much more is known about those various life forms, that adversely affect our crops and these have usually become referred to as 'pests & diseases'. Please bear in mind this book is not a comprehensive manual of these, as any specialist grower will know. This is more a collection of notes others made that they believed show relationships between plants and other living things, their 'co-lives'.

Introduction to Volume 1. Plants, their good & bad companions and worst weeds

Gardeners have long observed some plants do better with certain plants nearby, and worse with others. Indeed with so many thousands of different plants in near infinite combinations it would seem most strange if none ever did interact in some way other than competing for the same resources.

All plants compete with their neighbours by abstracting air, light, water and nutrients more or less effectively from their shared environment. Companion planting is about how plants also gain advantage over their neighbours by adding substances into their environment, deliberately or inadvertently, altering their competitors performance.

To give our crops optimum conditions it is considered sensible to control weeds. Obviously it's more effective to know and eliminate the more pernicious weeds than relatively benign ones. And now this must include other crops or flowers growing nearby that are acting much as extremely pernicious weeds.

Certain plants, including many common weeds, are far more deleterious than just usual competition would suggest, including many Asian and American weeds not yet familiar plants to the European grower. It's important to know of their effects as being weeds they may soon arrive on our shores if not here already. Likewise we need to know of any other related members (of the same genus), which we may already cultivate or have growing native, as these are very likely to employ and exhibit similar effects. Traditional companion planting was putting plants together that aided one another, or got on together. This is helpful. But it's more crucial to know which plants are hostile to any others presence. This especially so with crops where we must be aware which weeds are particularly pernicious because the germination and yields are heavily reduced in worst cases.

It's possible that the very worst weeds, from the point of view of loss of crops, are invisible, often remains of a prior crop, or residues from a nearby plant imagined innocuous whilst 'poisoning' the soil.

Introduction to Volume 2. Plants and Lepidoptera; the caterpillars and thus the butterflies these plants support

There are many books and sources recommending various flowers to 'feed the butterflies' and 'bring in more butterflies'. However most fail on one major point- you cannot have a butterfly on a flower without its larva eating the foliage of that or another plant! Providing a few more nectar sources does indeed feed the butterflies, but really does not increase their numbers or diversity. In fact you are just drawing them from elsewhere.

If we really want to have more butterflies we must also provide exactly those suitable plants that can feed their respective larvae, caterpillars, grubs, worms and miners.

Most larvae have a range of possible food plants and some will eat almost anything. We do not need alter our methods by much to help these especially the latter and if we grow any of their favourite plants we will almost certainly increase their numbers.

However some larvae are very particular and will not eat the wrong species let alone a different genus. To encourage such 'difficult' butterflies and moths then we must cultivate exactly the 'correct' plants to feed their larvae. These are most often native plants, or garden forms of these. However it would be foolish to encourage those Lepidoptera that also damage our crop plants, fortunately these are relatively few.

Introduction to Volume 3. Plants & their other co-lives: associated insects, fauna, nematodes, bacteria & fungi large and small

Crops do not exist independently in isolation but are a minute part of a huge intricate web of lives, animal and vegetable, big and small. This ecological mix involves almost all and every life on our planet and is continually in flux and evolution. Every living thing is jostling for living space and resources and needs to find its niche. In this melee some have become entwined with others, inter-dependent or actually reliant.

In nature associations have formed over time to fit local environmental conditions. Bogs, heaths, woodlands and meadows are examples of different plant communities. These are combinations of plants most suited to those conditions, and each other, and with all the other forms of life that live with and on those plants. There are not just lives that survive by eating certain plants but more lives that live by eating those, and others who dispose of the excreta and dead bodies, all recycling everything back to plants through the soil.

In farms and gardens we create an artificial mix of plants that could never be found in nature with our imagining each has no or little effect on another save that of straight competition. We also then regard most of their naturally associated life forms, their co-lives, that gain entry as unwelcome intruders or worse as 'pests and diseases'. Only the bigger and prettier ones are seen as 'wildlife' which needs 'encouraging'.

To help our crops we 'need' to control some of these other plants and co-lives as our un-natural mix does not create the automatic checks and balances found in long standing plant communities. We need to understand more fully this micro-ecology, that is which other flora and fauna are inter-acting with our chosen plants.

○ Key to text on the naming of plants and co-lives

Plant A-Z entries are alphabetical in Latin, eg. Acer followed by species under discussion, so Acer campestre. Then follows the common name(s) in capitals. Thus Acer campestre, FIELD MAPLE. Latin names are always started with a capital.
Common names of other plants and co-lives embedded in the text are entered without initial capitals unless important to the case in question.
Where alternative common and Latin names derived from old reference books, are recognised as such, these are entered spaced with **/** as in **Galium** aparine, GOOSE-GRASS / CLEAVERS.
Some serious confusion occurs as Latin names keep being changed, this adding a huge level of complexity when extracting references from older texts.
With Lepidoptera the foliage is usually the part eaten by the caterpillar / larva and the plant is said to Sustain it, with really pestilential larva the plant is said to Suffer it, if other parts are eaten these are noted after and in brackets thus (seeds) (flowers). Where a plant is thought the only sustainer this is emphasized, as are one of two or three sustainers and the alternatives.

Although great effort has been made to determine the exact species and variety under discussion many notes have necessarily been gleaned from old literature where a then-common common-name was used. So occasionally there will be 'wrong' identifications. Most probably this will be the substitution of a widespread species or variety in place of an originally local one employing the same or similar. (eg. references to 'Chamomile' have often proved misnomer or misidentification).

Also bear in mind that although only a particular genus and or species may be noted as having a certain association there is a very strong probability that other species in the same genus will have the same or similar associations so far gone unrecorded.

This work is offered in good faith but I cannot accept any responsibility for losses incurred by your interpretation and practice if some piece proves erroneous. (After all, will you be sending me shares of increased profits?)

Please accept my apologies for what I am sure must be many errors and omissions, and please let me know so the next edition can be corrected – bobflowerdew@bobflowerdew.com.uk

A-Z

- ○ **Actinidia deliciosa, KIWI**

Plants naturally dioecious and need one male to seven females, modern varieties may be self fertile.
Very vigorous climbers though can be spur pruned and espalier trained.
Fruits contain enzyme that prevents setting of jellies unless first cooked.
Fruits contain a fungicidal protein that inhibits Grey mould Botrytis cinerea and has been made into sprays to protect other plants.

- ○ **Agropyron repens, COUCH / WITCH / TWITCH / QUACK GRASS et al.**

Common tough grass weed, disappears from regularly cut sward.
Edible roots have been dried, ground, baked and eaten.
Suppressed by tomatoes, rape /colza and Tagetes minuta.
Reduces wheat yields by blocking uptake of phosphates, this occurs despite fertilizer applications.
Decaying roots encourage Fusarium culmorum which may then cause Foot rot and stunting in barley crops.

Inhibits germination and growth of alfalfa, curly cress, French & navy beans, and soya beans, thought to do so by inhibiting their rhizobium / Legume symbiosis.

Stems galled by hymenopteran gall-wasp Aulacidea hieracii / Aylax / sabaudi / graminis / Cynips which over-winter in the gall.

The inflorescence stalk is attacked by Dipteron chloropid Chlorops taeniopus Gout fly / Ribbon-footed corn-fly which lays eggs on the leaves or stalks, the larvae get into the shoots which thicken and form cigar shaped galls, the flower fails and the fly after hatching moves to alternate host, often barley.

Sustains 20 Lepidoptera larva.

One of two sustainers of 2: Beautiful Gothic Leucochlaena hispida / oditis other being Poa, and Marbled Minor Procus strigilis (inside stems) other being Dactylis.

One of three sustainers of 2: Essex Skipper Thymelicus lineola others being Brachypodium pinnatum and Phleum pratense, and Dark Arches Apamea monoglypha / polyodon others being Dactylis glomerata and Poa annua.

Also sustains: Dusky Brocade Apamea obscura / gemina / remissa, Speckled Wood / Wood Argus Pararge negeria, Wall butterfly Pararge megera, Grayling Satyrus semele, Hedge Brown / Gatekeeper Maniola tithonus, Meadow Brown Maniola jurtina, Ringlet Aphantopus hyperantus, Large Skipper Ochlodes venata / sylvanus, Drinker Philudoria potatoria, Lunar Yellow Underwing Triphaena orbona / subsequa, Common Wainscot Leucania pallens, White Point Leucania albipuncta, Orange Wainscot / Brown-line Bright-eye Leucania conigera, Slender Brindle Apamea scolopacina, Common Rustic Apamea secalis / oculea / didyma (inside stems), and Dusky Sallow Eremobia ochroleuca (on seeds).

○ Agrostis canina, BENT GRASS

This in particular, though other grasses as well, harbours the Reed-mace fungus Epichloe typhina. Sustains Antler Cerapteryx graminis.

○ Agrostis stolonifera, FIORIN

This species is eaten most readily by cows, horses and sheep.

- ### Agrostis vulgaris, FINE BENT / COMMON BENT

Found on poor dry sandy soils, eaten by Welsh sheep but not readily by cattle.

- ### Alliums

The Onion family, related to the lilies these usually form bulbs and many are used for culinary purposes; onions, leeks, shallots, garlic and chives.

Alliums are thus amongst the most effective good companions for many plants but do NOT get on with most Legumes, so keep them away from beans (Phaseolus and Vicia) and peas, and I am also concerned about Alliums following these in rotation and vice versa.

These have a strong smell helping hide other plants from pests, and as these accumulate sulphur they're considered to have fungicidal effects. Chives are often grown under roses for this purpose and hide the bare lower stems into the bargain.

Reputed to repel moles, you should be so lucky.

- ### Allium ascalonicum, SHALLOTS

Most unhappy of family with peas and beans. Plantains should not be allowed nearby as harbour Shallot aphids Myzus ascalonius which also move to strawberries.

○ Allium cepa, ONIONS

Do not press the sets in place as this damages the basal plate; make a raised mound of soil around the set holding it there till it's rooted, this helps deter worms too.

And DO NOT bend the necks down to 'help ripening' as this just lets in rots, particularly Neck rot which appears later if the crop is stored in stagnant conditions.

When mature onions are swelling and ripening it's beneficial to let the weeds grow as this takes up spare moisture and nutrients particularly Nitrogen and the bulbs then keep better.

The mutual detestation of beans and onions is well known, peas do not get on well with these but Brassicas do. Beet, tomatoes, lettuce grow well mutually with them as may strawberries. This strange looking combination always raises an eyebrow although the onions grow well and help prevent moulds on the strawberries. Summer savory is beneficial to onions. Chamomile aids when in small amounts.

Chrysanthemums planted close to onions or even in the soil onions had previously grown in grow smaller and flower prematurely.

Germination is inhibited by crimson clover, berseem clover, Johnson grass, Digera alternifolia, and hairy vetch. Purple nutsedge inhibits growth. Yields seriously reduced by N. American weeds Amaranthus palmeri and Johnson grass.

Onions or their extracts may deter Colorado beetles. Onion extracts have proved efficacious at preventing the hatching of many insect eggs.

Onion Fly Delia / Hylemyia antiqua attacks seedlings but plants from sets are older and tougher so often escape damage. The eggs are laid on the neck of the bulb, the maggots hatch in a week and destroy the roots causing flagging and yellowing then pupate overwinter in the soil there may be up to three generations.

All Alliums suffer from Pea eelworm nematode when their leaves swell and distort, and their bulbs crack and rot.

In cool wet years onion and shallot leaves will yellow and die, or simply look awful with a light greyish felt of Downy mildew Perenospora destructor this often comes in on the sets; do not use any that are soft.

Neck rot Botrytis alii appears in storage, grey mould on the outside with brown rotting inside, the fungus gets in through damage when the leaves are withering.

Onion Smut Urocystis cepulae is a notifiable disease, starts with greyish blackish spots and streaks on the leaves of seedlings which then twist and distort and black spores ooze from under bulb scales, may attack other Alliums as well.

Bright orange spots are Onion Rust Puccinia porri which rarely does much damage to older plants but kills seedlings, more of a problem for leeks and chives.

If plants wilt without obvious damage, with yellowing and die back and leaves then come away when pulled but there are no maggots eating the roots, and if there is a white mould covering the base with black dots then it is the dreaded White Rot Sclerotium cepivorum. Once this gets in (do not use cheap or culinary quality shallots and garlic for sets) it is impossible to be rid of and the ground needs resting for a decade from all Alliums, burn every infected plant and the soil around it. It can spread sideways in the soil over five yards in a year, much further if carried on boots or implements.

○ Allium porrum, LEEKS

Need unbelievably moist abundantly rich soil to thrive.

Cut tips off transplants to stop worms pulling the trailing leaves into their holes, then align transplants so leaves all face same way.

Not so miserable with beans as the other Alliums.

Leeks like the company of onions and grow well with celery and carrots.

Leeks intermixed with carrots decrease attacks of Carrot Root flies.

Said to help hide Brassicas from pigeons, though I doubt this.

Onion rust Puccinia porri bothers leeks more than it does onions and causes yellow or reddish spots and streaks which kills leaves and stunts plants.

White Tip Phytophthora porri causes ends of leaves to wither and turn white, the leaf margins may distort and water soaked areas form with loss of vigour and crop.

○ Allium sativum, GARLIC

The most pungent of the onion family and an accumulator of sulphur which may explain very ancient reputation for discouraging fungal pathogens.

Plant cloves in the autumn for bigger yields and do not put them too deep.

Garlic emulsion kills aphids and onion flies, it has also been used against codling moths, snails, root maggots, Japanese beetles, carrot root fly and peach leaf curl.

The cloves put in with grain discourage weevils. Garlic is not as pretty as chives as a companion but is especially good for roses and fruit trees, and mutually beneficial with vetches.

○ Allium schoenoprasum, CHIVES

Often grown with other plants to reduce fungal diseases, particularly blackspot on roses and scab on apples but be patient as it takes three years to take effect.

These and their extracts discourage aphids from chrysanthemums, sunflowers and tomatoes and benefit carrots.

Chive sprays have been used against both Downy and Powdery mildew on cucumbers and gooseberries.

○ Alopecuris pratensis, MEADOW FOX-TAIL

Sheep and horses enjoy eating this grass but cows do not.

○ Amaranthus, AMARANTH

Edible highly nutritious semi-tropical annuals, leaves often used as salading or spinach and the seeds also eaten in many ways.
Needs hot summers to do well in UK.
Host plant to ground beetles.

○ Amaranthus leucocarpis, GRAIN AMARANTH

Exudates inhibit germination of many weeds, and crops.
Alfalfa and rye exudates inhibit both its germination and seedling growth.
Pollen from sweet corn / maize may seriously hinder its growth.

o Anthoxanthum odoratum, SWEET-SCENTED VERNAL GRASS

Eaten but not readily by cows, horses and sheep.

o Apium graveolens, CELERY

Edible but tough and bitter unless you have a rich constantly moist soil, grow celeriac instead as celery is a difficult crop. It must never dry out, is prone to bolting, suffers badly from slugs, and also needs blanching.
Self blanching types are hardly so and tougher textured.
Celery seed is a good but under-used condiment.
Celery grows well with beans, tomatoes and best of all with leeks probably mostly because these like the same rich moist conditions.
If left to flower celery attracts many beneficial insects especially predatory wasps.
Foliage may be attacked by Celery & Parsnip fly Tephritis / Trypeta onopordinis this conflated with Celery fly Philophylla heraclei, which lays on the underside of the leaves and raises tunnels and blisters inside the leaf blade in which the maggots feed, leaving to pupate in the soil and overwinter, up to three generations a year.
One of many sub-races of microscopic Stem eelworm nematodes Ditylenchus dipsaci causes thickening of the leaf bases and crown with loss of vigour.

Celery may suffer Root rot Phoma apiicola causing worst case plants to fall off at ground level, this is seed borne.

Soft rot Bacterium carotovorum sometimes gets in through damage and the inside just moulds away.

Celery Leaf Spot / Celery Rust Septoria apii is serious once introduced, on seed or by debris, small yellow brown spots spread from outer to inner leaves then all over with a totally debilitated if not dead plant. Can be discouraged from starting with tea made from nettles and equisetum.

- ## Apium graveolens rapaceum, CELERIAC

Near identical to celery but with swollen edible root not stalk thus different co-lives interact.

Easier to grow well than celery, but still needs constant moisture, remove lowest leaves and any surface roots to make the crown swell.

Grows best in rich soil following Legumes, especially after green manure of vetches. Grows well between rows of runner beans if kept moist.

Good companion with leeks which are tolerated by runner beans and make a trio where moisture is abundant. Celeriac can do well with tomatoes and most Brassicas.

Sustains Swallow-tail Papilio machaon.

Sustains damage to roots from Small / Garden Swift moth Hepialus lupulinus, which also attacks beans, parsnip, lettuce, potato, strawberry and grass roots. Soft rot sometimes gets in through other damage and then the inside moulds away.
Rust and leaf spot disease are serious once introduced (often on seed).

- ## Armoracia rusticana, HORSERADISH

Edible root, especially good grated with garlic, chilli, mustard and cider vinegar to make a warming sauce! The leaf spine bruised and retted for a fornight or so self bleaches into good twine.
Aids potatoes, the Chinese grow these together, but as it's difficult to be rid of horseradish it's better grown in large pots or woven plastic sacks half buried in the potato bed so it can't escape. The perforated stainless steel drums that come out of washing machines make good confinements.
According to Gerard horseradish is bad for grapevines though I've seen no problem.
The tea, of the foliage or root not specified, has been used against Brown rot in apples.
In US used against Blister beetles and Colorado beetles.
Sustains / suffers: Green-veined White Pieris napi, and Garden Carpet Xanthorhoe fluctuata.

The roots may be attacked by Black rot Pseudomonas campestris, the same as attacks turnips and seakale, if cut the roots show blackened rings, the foliage is often also seen to suffer in vigour.

The foliage also gets White Blister from glistening white pustules of Cystopus candidus more commonly found on Brassicas.

Leaf Spots are most likely Pale Leaf Spot caused by fungus Ramularia armoraciae with whitish spots which may lose their centres becoming shot-holed.

○ **Asparagus officinalis, ASPARAGUS**

Originally of maritime regions, traditionally grown in vineyards of Beaujolais as this likes conditions under grapes, and berries said to distract birds but I do not observe this to be so as these last long into winter.

Tomato foliage smell can protect it from asparagus beetle, while a root secretion from asparagus kills Trichodorus, a nematode that attacks tomato roots. Tomato and asparagus both like basil so make a happy trio where warm enough. Parsley can do well with asparagus but only where it can get the moisture it thrives on. Potatoes do grow remarkably well near asparagus though it's then hard to extract the crop without damaging roots.

However asparagus residues will reduce the germination of tomatoes, and lettuces, and reduce growth of lettuces and barley. Onions and possibly other Alliums are also disliked.

Seriously allelopthic to itself so asparagus seedlings seldom germinate where plants are or have been and it is difficult to establish even pot grown plants in old beds.

Asparagus Beetle Crioceris asparagi larvae cause serious damage, a multitude of tiny grubs eat the foliage down to the ribs, the adult is pretty, black with orange markings.

Reddy orange blisters on the stems and leaves browning before autumn is Asparagus rust Puccinia asparagi, overwinters as black streaks on the withered stems and reappears as rusty powder on the summer fern.

A rusty, brownish or purplish colour to the roots and crown which then die away indicate fungal Violet root rot / Copper-web Helicobasidium purpureum which also attacks beet, carrot, parsnip, potatoes, clover, alfalfa, and several weeds.

o Avena eliator, TALL OAT GRASS

Does best on clay, disliked by cows, sheep and especially by horses.

o Avena fatua, WILD OATS

Exudates reduce wheat yields significantly, and seriously reduce growth of sweet corn / maize, mustard and Pennisetum americanum.

o Avena flavescens, YELLOW OAT

GRASS

Eaten by sheep and cows, yields apparently often doubled by application of calcerous manures.

○ Avena sativa, OATS

A cereal, and weed often found in with other cereals. Oats reduce to 4% ashes which contain 21% potash, little soda, 10% lime, 8% magnesia, 4% iron oxide, 0.4% manganese oxide, 51% phosphoric acid, negligible sulphuric acid, 4% silica and 0.6% chlorine. Oats make a good mixed fodder crop for stock at two to one with vetches or beans, best if sown after the beans have germinated.

These and occasionally other grains were sown in the bottom of holes for trees, whether for the heat of germination, exudates or by-products is not known. Mouldy oats aid peach trees but oat root secretions may be unfriendly to apricots.

Of 3,000 oat varieties tested 25 produced an exudate that inhibited cruciferous weeds.

Oats suppress fat hen and are suppressed by thistles and sunflowers. Exudates and run off from oats suppress germination of sweet corn / maize.

The Frit fly Oscinis frit the eggs laid in spring hatch to tiny legless larvae which eat into the growing point and the plant is stunted even killed, leaves are stunted and crops suffer, there can be up to three generations in a year, then larvae overwinter in grasses, also attacks maize.

The Stem Eelworm Tylenchus devastatrix of clover has alternate host of oats and especially of the old tulip-rooted oats, so never follow or precede oats with clovers.

<u>One of three sustainers</u> Flounced Rustic Luperina testacea (on roots) others being Hordeum and Triticum.

Also sustains: Rosy Minor Procus literosa (in stems), Rosy Rustic Hydraecia micacea (in stems), and Brighton Wainscot Oria musculosa (in stems).

In soil containing Penicillium griseofulvum the plants take up the antibiotic griseofulvin and become seriously retarded.

o Avena ubescens, OAT-GRASS

Sustains: Beaded Chestnut Agrochola lychnidis / pistacina, and Dusky Sallow Eremobia ochroleuca (seeds).

o Beta vulgaris, BEET / RED BEET / BEETROOT / LEAF BEAT / PERPETUAL SPINACH / SWISS CHARD / SUGAR BEET

Originating from maritime regions these need trace elements more than most crops and thrive on seaweed products. Good mineral accumulators, up to one quarter of leaf ash content can be Magnesium.

Any shortage of Manganese especially in dry conditions may cause yellowing and poor growth.

If soil is deficient in Boron may develop Heart rot with a brown centre as leaves wilt and turn black.

If beets start to bolt and form flower stems said these should be pulled to stop them 'encouraging' others.

Beets do well with most beans (Phaseolus and Vicia) though not with the runners which shade them. They like lettuce, onions and get on with Brassicas especially kohlrabi. However the Brassica related weeds charlock and wild mustard are particularly detrimental.

Beet usefully hinder corn cockle seeds germinating.

The most troublesome co-lives by far are birds eating seeds, seedlings and younger leaves.

Beet are frequently bothered by Black aphids, Flea beetles and the Pea eelworm nematode.

The Mangold fly Pegomyia hyoscyami / betae has small whitish larvae which tunnel and blister the leaves which drop early, the larvae pupate in the soil and emerge three weeks later giving three generations in a year.

Leaves may be eaten by Beet Carrion Beetle Silpha opaca which also consumes dead animals and general garbage.

Sustains: Lepidoptera larva Silver Gamma / Y Moth Plusia gamma, and Nutmeg Hadena trifolii / chenopodii.

Soil bacteria Enterobacter, Klebsiella, Citrobacter, Flavobacterium, Achromobacter, Arthrobacter and Pseudomonas reduce germination and seriously hinder growth and increase infection by root colonizing fungi.

Leaf spots Cercospora beticola cause brown spots with purple borders grey in middle turn to small holes.

Heart rot mentionned above causes the leaves to turn black and die back, crown first then outer leaves, then the root rots, remember this may be induced by Boron deficiency.

If the root and or stem below the seed leaves turns black and dies first it was more likely Black Leg Phoma betae, Pythium aphamidermatum and Corticum solani, several diseases with similar symptoms, and all are seed borne.

Rough patches are just common Scab.

Downy mildew Personospora farinosa causes younger leaves to thicken with a greyish mat on the underside, then yellow, brown and blacken with loss of growth, spread both on the seed and from debris and litter.

The underground parts get attacked by fungus Urophlyctis leproides which galls the flesh into large swellings.

Beets and chards are attacked by same Violet root rot that kills asparagus and carrots.

Rhizomania is a new disease of sugar beet increasingly rendering East Anglian fields un-usable for the whole family, the roots proliferate but work ineffectively, spread on soil, so beware when walking out not to bring it home. (I suggest we breed high sugar parsnips or even carrots, these were roots first used to produce sugar but never developed further when sugar beet were found the sweeter.)

Virus Yellows is also more common in farming with sugar beet than in garden beets, it's spread by aphids Myzus persicae and Aphis fabae, the leaves develop patches of yellow turning orangey red, mostly on the edges, the leaves then become brittle and break up on handling, the growth is poor so are resultant crops.

Beet Curly Top virus is spread by leaf-hoppers and also invades Cucurbits, beans, tomatoes and many other plants.

Beet Pseudo-Yellows virus, spread by whiteflies, also invades Cucurbits and many other plants.

Beet Western Yellows virus, spread by aphids, also invades many other plants especially lettuce.

Garden-beet mosaic also attacks spinach.

o **Borago officinalis, BORAGE**

Edible in moderation as spinach, flowers used in Pimms.

A good accumulator of minerals for compost it makes an excellent liquid feed often better for many plants than comfrey as richer in Magnesium and Nitrogen and less likely to cause chlorosis.

One of few plants that will grow in foul water.
One of the best bee plants.
Excellent green manure and exudates hinder germination of many seeds.
Benefits strawberries.
Used to discourage Japanese beetles and tomato hornworms.
Sustains: Queen of Spain Fritillary Argynnis lathonia, Crimson-speckled Utetheisa pulchella, and may sustain Bright Wave Sterrha ochrata / ochrearia.

- ○ **Brachypodium pinnatum, HEATH FALSE-BROME GRASS**

Sustains 7 Lepidoptera larva.
<u>Sole sustainer of</u> Lulworth Skipper Thymelicus action / actaeon.
<u>One of two sustainers</u> Straw Dot Rivula sericealis other being Carex.
<u>One of three sustainers</u> Essex Skipper Thymelicus lineola others being Agropyron repens and Phleum.
Also sustains: Grayling Satyrus semele, Meadow Brown Maniola jurtina / janira, Small Heath Coenonympha pamphilus, and Small Skipper Thymelicus sylvestris / linea / thaumus.

- ○ **Brachypodium sylvaticum, SLENDER FALSE-BROME GRASS**

Sustains 8 Lepidoptera larva.

One of two sustainers of 2: Chequered Skipper Carterocephalus palaemon / paniscus other being Bromus, and Straw Dot Rivula sericealis other being Carex.

Also sustains: Speckled Wood / Wood Argus Pararge negeria, Wall butterfly Pararge megera, Ringlet Aphantopus hyperantus, Large Skipper Ochlodes venata / sylvanus, Small Skipper Thymelicus sylvestris / linea / thaumus, and Feathered Ear Pachetra sagittigera / leucophaea.

- o **Brassicas**

The cabbage family are highly bred and very specialised needing rich soil with plenty of lime. In acid soils they become prey to Club root, see below, and also to Whiptail where the leaves become reduced to straps or whips and the growing point may be lost, this is a deficiency not a disease, cured by adding seaweed products or Molybdenum salts to the soil.

Most Brassicas especially cabbage and cauliflower also need Magnesium or the leaves can become pale, marbled with a purplish hue.

Sometimes Brassicas suffer frost damage which looks like a disease with whitish patches going brown with the leaves dying.

They benefit from herbs such as chamomile, dill, peppermint, rosemary and sage. Do well with peas, celery, potatoes, onions and dwarf beans but not with rue, runner beans, lettuce or strawberries.

Under-sowing Brassicas with clover or bird's foot trefoil reduces aphid infestations without harming yields.

Interplanting Brassicas with French beans significantly reduce pest levels on both.

Should not follow alfalafa or be grown with this as alfalfa exudates inhibit growth of cabbages.

Yields seriously reduced by US weed Johnson grass and by Artemesias.

Brassicas give off strongly allelopathic substances that seriously inhibit wheat (in order of strength, B. campestris, B. juncea, B. napus, B. nigra). Tomatoes are controversial, said to aid spring cabbage but their seasons barely touch.

Trials show that although you could successfully follow a broccoli crop with a cabbage crop but you couldn't follow one with cauliflowers due to inhibitory substances from the roots.

All Brassicas may inadvertently support colonies of spiders, earwigs, wood lice and other critters to little or no detriment and often to advantage as these predate each other, process material or act as pollinators.

Slugs and snails are another matter.

Young plants often damaged or destroyed by cutworms, wireworms and cockchafers, see Cutworms and ground caterpillars et al.

The Turnip sawfly Athalia rosae is a major pest on the continent of turnips and oilseed rape and could re-invade the UK.

Far worse is Cabbage root fly Erioischia Brassicae / Delia / Anthomyia radicum, this eats the roots of all Brassicas, the females consume nectar of Cow parsley Anthriscus sylvestris so are most prevalent when this is flowering, the Brassica plants turn reddish purple once attacked. These flies can be lured to traps containing swede root juice as bait. Interplanting lettuce, clover or Tagetes marigolds reduces infestations. Carefully fitted collars of felt or similar at ground level stop the fly climbing down the stem to the soil and prevent her laying eggs, there are two or more generations a year. Heavy attacks of aphids deter this fly and apparently the Garden Pebble moth caterpillar Evergestis forficalis exudes a deterrent chemical in its frass. Rove and Ground beetles also help control the root fly by eating the eggs and the Rove Aleochara Bilineata eats large numbers of the pupae. However the major parasite is a small wasp Idiomorpha rapae which lays eggs in the pupae which the larvae feed inside.

The Radish Fly Anthomyia floralis, also damages roots and lower stalk, especially of turnips, this may also breed in exposed fresh dung.

Most Brassicas suffer from Cabbage Fly Anthomyia Brassicae which is also known as Snowy Fly / Cabbage Powdered-Wing / Cabbage Whitefly Aleurodes Brassicae / proletella / cheledonii (and also very often wrongly confused with the Glasshouse whitefly Trialeurodes vaporariorum which is sometimes found outdoors on other crops). The tiny larvae, in huge numbers, have a serious effect depriving the plants of sap and exuding honeydew which then coats leaves and becomes infested with Sooty mould which 'mess up' the plants, as the complete life cycle is only a fortnight there can be up to ten generations a year.

Flea beetles Phyllotreta atra, P. nemorum, P. undulate and other spp. are small, black or yellow striped, eat the young leaves and cause serious loss of young plants, deterred by damper conditions and presence of tomatoes, the adults are the problem, the larvae live in the soil on plant roots doing little harm.

The Swede midge Contarinia nasturtii attacks all Brassicas despite the name, the grubs are small creamy and found on the leaf stalks of plants that have gone Blind, ie the central growing point is destroyed and the plant becomes useless, the wounds may also allow diseases to infect as well.

Mealy Cabbage Aphis Brevicoryne Brassicae is blueish grey, usually on underside of leaves, damages growth and 'messes up' the plants, they overwinter as eggs on the stems, are parasitised by tiny Chalcid wasps Aphidius spp. which lay an egg in each aphid which the larva eats before emerging leaving the now empty light brown skin through a small round hole.

The Peach potato aphid Myzus persicae, Shallot Aphis M. ascalonicus, Onion thrips Thrips tabaci, Cabbage thrips Thrips angusticeps, Brassica shield bug Eurydema oleracea, and the Common flower bug Anthocoris nemorum may all be found but seldom doing serious damage.

A Coleopteran weevil, Cabbage / Turnip Gall Weevil, Ceuthorrhynchus pleurostigma / sulcicollis / assimilis a.k.a. 'Turnip and Cabbage gall weevil' has brown headed white grubs which form marble sized swellings on the roots of all Brassicas, may seriously harm growth in young small plants and older ones and the larval exit holes allow in other infections. This can be widespread in an area as it also attacks Arabis, turnips, cabbages, swedes, wild radish and charlock. The damage is often confused with that of Club Root, see below, however cutting open galls reveals maggots and not a smelly slimy mess.

Various leaf and stem miners may be present: Cabbage Leaf miner Phytomyza rufipes, Phytomyza horticola, and the Cabbage Stem weevil Ceutorrhynchus quadridens live in most Brassicas especially spring sown crops. The Cabbage Stem Flea beetle Psylliodes chrysocephala grubs tunnel into the stems of young plants causing them to fail, particularly bothering cauliflowers. Turnip Stem weevil C. contractus is found in the stem, veins and midribs. Turnip Mud beetle Helophorus spp. larvae may be found in winter mining the stems. Mustard / Watercress beetle Phaedon cochleariae larvae may be found in summer.

Pollen beetles Meligethes spp. are more of a problem for oilseed rape and for those growing Brassicas for seed. Likewise the Rape Winter Stem weevil Ceutorhynchus picitarsis is only a major problem on over-wintering rape crops.

The Cabbage Seed weevil Ceutorhynchus assimilis female feeds on pollen first then eats the seeds in the seedpod and finally lays eggs which hatch inside and eat even more seeds. Worse, the damaged pods allow the Brassica Pod midge Dasyneura Brassicae to lay it's eggs and their larvae cause the pod to become bladder-like and spill any surviving seeds.

The shoot apex may be galled by Dipteron gall-midge Dasyneura sisymbrii / Cecidomyia barbarea, this arrests normal growth causing glossy swellings and lumps, often cream, pink or reddish, worst in floral parts, serious infestations can form what look much like small raspberries, often infests other cruciferae such as hedge mustard, creeping yellow cress, charlock and wild radish.

All these co-lives are inter-active, when all small white butterfly eggs and caterpillars were removed from a stand of collards the numbers of flea beetles Phyllotreta cruciferae increased, when these were removed another flea beetle Phyllotreta striolata increased.

Sustain / suffer a huge number of Lepidoptera larva: Silver Y moth Autographa gamma, Dot moth Melanchra persicariae, Flax tortrix moth Cnephasia interjectana, Tomato moth / Bright-line Brown-eye moth Lacanobia oleracea, Turnip moth Agrotis segetum, Garden Pebble moth Evergestis forficalis, Bright Wave Sterrha ochrata / ochrearia, Pearly Underwing Peridroma saucia, Garden Carpet moth Xanthorhoe fluctuata, Heart & Dart moth Agrotis exclamationis, Dark Swordgrass / Dark Dart Agrotis ipsilon, and fat, black striped larvae of Great Yellow Underwing Moth Noctua / Tryphaena pronuba (on roots and leaves).

Suffer: the Large Cabbage White Pieris Brassicae, which has black markings on creamy white wings, these lay yellow eggs in clusters of thirty to a hundred, caterpillars start greyish green but may become bright green with black markings or bluish green with three lines yellow and black spots when mature, they quit the plants to pupate nearby, the butterflies are deterred by tomatoes, thyme and by fake eggs or crushed eggs. Parasitised by small black braconid wasp Apanteles glomeratus, this lays eggs in caterpillar which eventually form up to thirty yellow cocoons around the poor critter having eaten it from the inside. However these are themselves parasitized by hyper-parasites, an even smaller metallic green wasp Tetrastichus galactopus and an Ichneumon wasp Lysibia nana. Apantales cocoons may be conflated with small yellow silky cocoons containing pupae of the Ichneumon fly Microgaster glomeratus who lays about sixty eggs in a Large White caterpillar parasitising it. Another Ichneumon Fly Pteromalus Brassicae lays up to two hundred and fifty eggs on the newly formed chrysalis parasitizing it.

These Lepidoptera caterpillars can be controlled with Bacillus thuriengiensis, found naturally in the soil or available commercially. As these caterpillars mostly damage the outer leaves they can do more harm to such as kales (which they seldom touch) and Portugese cabbage, Trouve conchuda, while with cabbage, cauliflower and broccolis the heads may escape almost unscathed, though obviously growing less well when the leaf area removed is significant. Suffer the similar Small White or Turnip Moth Artogeia / Pieris rapae, their eggs are laid singly becoming velvet green caterpillars with three yellow lines and NO black spots.

Suffer the Green Veined White P. napi, their eggs laid singly, grub velvet green with a row of red to yellow breathing holes on sides. These both do much damage to the heads of cabbage, cauliflowers, broccolli as they eat into the middle. More of these caterpillars will be found on plants growing on their own than on those in stands of many.

Suffer the Cabbage moth Mamestra Brassicae whose fat brown caterpillars eat the inside of the heart each causing far more damage than other caterpillars which consume mostly outer leaves, the eggs are laid singly so hard to spot though the grub's greenish brown frass is easily found.

Also suffer the Diamond-back moth Plutella xylostella which has grey green caterpillars which feed on the leaf underside leaving the thin transparent upper skin and veins, these reach about half an inch long then pupate in cocoons on the leaves before emerging to start the next, of up to ten generations in a year.

Damping Off from Rhizoctonia solani kills small Brassica seedlings who wilt and die the stem collapsing at about ground level. Similar symptoms occur with Ascochyta spp. and Pythium spp. The spores live in the soil and attacks are worst with overcrowded plants in high humidity and with stagnant air.

Sawdust, even 1%, added to soils makes Brassica seedlings more susceptible to Pythium damping off.

Black Rot, Pseudomonas / Xanthomonas campestris bacterial invasion causes yellowing leaves with blackened veins, when cut stems show black dots in a ring, seen in warm wet years, mostly attacks cabbage and cauliflower may also spread to turnip, swede and seakale, often introduced on the seed but also soil borne.

Soft Rot, Bacterium carotovorum, slimy rotting, also attacks carrot, turnip, swede celery etc. often worse after plants frosted or over-fed.

Downy mildew Peronospora parasitica is most often found on seedlings, especially cauliflowers, raised under cover or in overcrowded high humidity conditions, soil borne this causes yellowing of the leaves with downy patches underneath, may kill seedlings or weaken them, also attacks the curds of cauliflowers and broccolis and can be pernicious on Brussel's sprouts.

Grey Mould, Botrytis cinerea, only too well known grey fluffy fungal mould, worst in humid conditions. Brassicas are exceedingly prone to slime fungal attacks of Clubroot disease / Finger & toe / Anbury, Plasmodiophora Brassicae, causing distorted swollen roots which rot inside and smell vile. If you do not have this in your soil NEVER bring in any Brassica plants or soil from infected allotments. Do without as once present this disease is almost incurable. Exudates and extracts from peppermint, summer savory and thyme can reduce infections of clubroot fungus, rhubarb has only a small effect, frequent short term green manuring with mustard may reduce infestation. Also attacks and lives on cruciferous weeds such as shepherds purse and charlock. Club root is much worse in wet heavy acid soils and less severe in lime containing ones.

Black Leg / Black Stem / Canker Phoma lingam fungal attack, spots on leaves, brownish purple to black cankers on stems at base cause roots to wilt and die, also attacks swedes, usually seed borne.

Leaf Spots / Ring Spots Mycosphaerella brassicola, brown spots with green border or rings, fungal attack on lower leaves, most often found in wetter counties and on broccolis, more of an appearance problem than actual damage.

White Blister Cystopis candidus fungal attacks cause glistening white blisters in spots or rings, often found on over-crowded plants especially Brussell's sprouts, also attacks radish, turnips etc. and cruciferous weeds. Ringspot virus causes small spots which start off pale green, may also cause distorted leave and yellowing, also attacks stocks, wallflowers, sweet rocket and Arabis where it affects flowers as well. Cauliflower mosaic virus causes the veins to stand out with the leaf blade between a yellowed or paler green, vigour is lost, this is spread by aphids Brevicoryne Brassicae and Myzus persicae, hosted by several weeds especially related cruciferae.

Turnip mosaic virus, also spread by aphids, also invades most cruciferous plants and lettuce.

o **Brassica alba / juncea / nigra / campestris, BROWN MUSTARD, (see also Sinapsis)**

What is sold as salad mustard may be the similar and much cheaper oilseed rape, true mustard is not as hardy and is killed by hard frosts.

It makes a good cover crop leaving soil in fine condition and can be used to attract many pests of Brassicas, then dug in or composted.

It should be added, at about 15%, when grassing down an orchard and is a corrective green manure on acid soils.

Gertrud Franck maintains that although mustard is a Brassica this is botanical classification rather than a close family relationship and that mustard can be used frequently as a green manure without any affect on rotations. This is controversial as most books on disease state mustard suffers from Clubroot, the most feared disease of Brassicas. However, if the mustard does not live for long and is incorporated or composted well before the disease can produce a new crop of spores, there is unlikely to be a problem. Mustard green manures will also help control nematodes.

Mustard improves yields of wheat when sown at rate of 12 kg/hectare.

Several weeds suppress mustard germinating: Datura species, Clerodendrum viscosum, Dicanthium annulatum, Cassia sophera and Crotolaria pallida all inhibit growth and or germination. The leachates of Clerodendrum even causing chlorosis, this also caused by leaf leachate of Pluchea lanceolata an Asian weed which then hinders growth. Croton bonplandianum exudates seriously reduce germination. Eragrostis poaeoides, another Asian weed, exudates inhibit germination then reduce growth as does Xanthium strumarium. Growth inhibited by wild oats and by leaf exudates of Chenopodium murale but mustard seed yield is increased by this lasts' infloresence exudates

o **Brassica chinensis, CHINESE GREENS / CABBAGE & PAK CHOI**

These need rich soil with almost bog conditions and sowing after midsummer to succeed.
Do well near Brussel's sprouts.
Germination hindered by exudates from Miscanthus. Seriously self inhibiting, and exudates inhibit lettuce and mustard, avidly eaten by flea beetle, slugs and aphids, so make good sacrificial and trap crops.
In the USA used as sacrificial for maize crops as it attracts their corn worms.

- ○ **Brassica napus oleifera, RAPE or COLZA**

Annual crop very much like mustard but which it should not be confused with. Grown for oil it gives about three tons of rough dry matter per acre containing about three to four hundred pounds of oil and over a quarter ton of mineral ash.

In UK oilseed rape strains usually derived from Swede rape, in Canada and Scandinavia from Turnip rape.

As a green manure it loosens heavy soil, it makes a good green manure / cover crop over-winter if not close in rotation with other Brassicas.

Suppressed by couch grass and wild mustards.

Both germination and growth seriously hindered by Striga densiflora weeds.

- ○ **Brassica napus / rapa napoBrassica, SWEDE**

Very similar to turnip but orange fleshed, prone to 'Crown gall' which has many points of similarity to cancer tumours in animals as it spreads forming tumours elsewhere than original site, caused by bacterium Agrobacterium / Bacillus / Phytomonas / Pseudomonas tumefaciens, which spreads to nearly twenty families of herbaceous and some woody plants.

Like cabbages and many cruciferous weeds swedes suffer slime-fungus attacks to their roots by Plasmodiophora Brassicae, the dreaded Club Root which forms finger like galls on the side branching roots.

○ Brassica oleraceae, COLLARDS

These are primitive cabbage plants grown for their small loose heads. Smaller but tougher than cabbages they're easier to grow especially in hot conditions though then often suffer from Flea beetles.

○ Brassica oleraceae, KALES

Another Brassica prone to the same pests and diseases but tougher than most and very hardy, will survive most UK winters.
Chopped fine and deep fried this is too often sold as 'seaweed' by perfidious merchants.

○ Brassica oleracea, KOHLRABI

A tough and disease resistant crop much like a turnip but easier and not as hot, should be more widely grown.
Dutch form Superschmeltz gets huge, stores well and good stock fodder.
Does not get on with tomatoes, strawberries, peppers or runner beans, fine with onions, beet and cucumber.

- **Brassica oleracea botrytis botrytis, CAULIFLOWER**

These are cauliflowers if they head up in the warmer months but the over-wintering ones are botanically broccolis.

The part we eat is an enormous multiple flowered head suspended in the bud stage. Any check or damage will lead to 'button' heads.

There are red and green cauliflowers and dwarf ones that take less space, these all require rich moist soil to do well, and as these are so highly bred sowing dates are critical!

Break and bend outer leaves over ripening heads to prevent white curds from yellowing.

Acid soils especially those lacking in trace elements may cause cauliflowers, and some other Brassicas, to develop thin spindly leaves called Whiptail, easily cured with seaweed sprays, Molybdenum salts and liming.

They're much the same in choice of companions as other Brassicas mainly disliking tomatoes and strawberries.

Rue has proved bad for cauliflowers.

The Cabbage Stem Flea beetle Psylliodes chrysocephala grubs tunnel into the stems of young plants causing them to fail.

- **Brassica oleracea/ botrytis cymosa,**

BROCCOLIS

Winter cauliflowers are usually broccolis as these are hardier than true cauliflowers. They are highly bred and require very rich conditions and heavy soil to form the swollen and immature lateral and terminal flower buds. The shape and texture of these heads makes pest problems more detrimental than for say cabbage where damaged outer leaves can be discarded.

- ## Brassica oleracea / botrytis cymosa, CALABRESE

These are varieties of tenderer broccoli with similar needs to cauliflowers.

- ## Brassica oleracea / capitata, CABBAGE

A cabbage is a terminal bud and to get it to swell without opening is a marvel of controlling nature. Constant unchecked growth in rich moist conditions is required. There are red versions; rubra, as well as white; alba, and Savoys; sabauda, which have crinkly leaves and are hardier than the others.

Ash contains 0.4% Potassium, 0.15% Phosphorus and 0.2% Calcium, and the plants need plenty of Magnesium or leaves pale and mottle and go purplish.

Most important, as with all Brassica family, is liming, rotation and avoid importing anything potentially carrying Club Root disease.

Avoid strawberries, and possibly cabbages may not get on with grapevines.

Aided and protected by herbs nearby: dill, mints, rosemary, sage, thyme, hyssop and chamomile.

One common companion idea was to plant wormwood or southernwood with cabbages to drive away the white butterflies. It works but the leaf exudations poison the soil and lowered yields significantly.

Germination and growth inhibited by Palmer amaranth.

Cabbages especially suffer from the Cabbage moth Mamestra Brassicae whose fat brown caterpillars eat the inside of the heart causing far more damage than other caterpillars which consume mostly outer leaves, the eggs are laid singly so hard to spot though the grub's greenish brown frass is easily found.

o **Brassica oleracea gemmifera, BRUSSEL'S SPROUTS**

These may be bad for grapevines.

One of the hardier Brassicas, they have the family tendencies with a liking for really firm soil, in windy areas tie the matured plants at the top to make tripods.

White Blister Cystopis candidus fungal attacks cause glistening white blisters in spots or rings, is often found on over-crowded plants, also attacks radish, turnips etc. and cruciferous weeds.

- ## Brassica rapa rapa TURNIP

Not Swedes, B. napa / rapa napoBrassica, which are Swedish turnips which have a different sweeter less hot taste and yellow flesh. Turnips are smaller, whiter, quicker to crop and get hotter to taste, need moist rich soil.

May develop a brown centre to the root if the soil is deficient in Boron.

Another of the cabbage family with all their traits, these get on well with peas and are benefited by vetches, especially hairy tare, which helps distract aphids.

They do not like hedge mustard or knotweeds and tobacco root exudates seriously hinder germination and growth.

Many co-lives are named Turnip this or that as they were first noticed on turnips but interact with most Brassicas so their entries are with the respective Brassicas.

Flea beetles Phyllotreta spp. are often an especial problem best cleared by waving sticky flypaper close above the seedlings.

Cabbage root fly Erioischia Brassicae / Delia / Anthomyia radicum, eats the roots of all Brassicas, but as it tunnels through the swollen edible part of a turnip becomes more of a problem and sometimes does the same with Swedes, the females consume nectar of Cow parsley Anthriscus sylvestris so are most prevalent when this is flowering, the leaves often turn reddish purple if plant is attacked. These flies can be lured to traps containing Swede root juice as bait. Interplanting lettuce, clover or Tagetes marigolds reduces infestations. Heavy attacks of aphids deter this fly and oddly the Garden Pebble moth caterpillar Evergestis forficalis apparently exudes a deterrent chemical in it's frass. Rove and Ground beetles also control the fly by eating the eggs. Sometimes the Turnip Gall weevil makes lumpy swellings which disclose a whitish legless grub, this may be confused with Clubroot if the maggot is not seen.

Turnips suffer from Soft rot where some damage allows disease in to rot the heart out.

Radish scab Streptomyces scabies makes scabby patches on the skin but seldom does serious harm, attacks may be reduced by mixing grass clippings or other rich organic material into the soil when sowing.

Black Leg / Black Stem / Canker Phoma lingam is a fungal attack, spots on leaves, brownish purple to black cankers on stems at base cause roots to wilt and die, also attacks swedes, usually seed borne.

- Brassica sinapis, see Sinapis, CHARLOCK

- Briza media, COMMON QUAKING-GRASS

Sustains Slender Brindle Apamea scolopacina.

- Briza minor, LESSER QUAKING-GRASS

Sustains Slender Brindle Apamea scolopacina.

- Bromus arvensis, FIELD BROME-GRASS

Sustains Shaded Broad-Bar Ortholitha chenopodiata / limitata / mensuraria, Wall butterfly Pararge megera, Marbled White Melanargia galathea, and Meadow Brown Maniola jurtina.

- Bromus ramosus, ROUGH BROME-GRASS

One of two sustainers Chequered Skipper Carterocephalus palaemon / paniscus other being Brachypodium.

Also sustains: Wall butterfly Pararge megera, Marbled White Melanargia galathea, and Meadow Brown Maniola jurtina.

- ○ **Capsicum, HOT / SWEET / BELL PEPPERS**

Tender plants that although prone to aphids themselves are source of hot chilli pepper made from dried fruit and seeds effective at discouraging many pests. Mammals feel the burning sensation caused by capsaicin however birds do not taste it.

Some chillis have root exudates that inhibit Fusarium diseases.

These like basil which grows well with them, but not kohlrabi or radishes, and often grown with okra for convenience.

Inhibited by Asian weed Bothriochloa pertusa. Digera alternifolia, another Asian weed, markedly decreases germination.

Over thirty viruses are known to cause losses such as Potato virus, Tobacco Etch virus, Pepper Mottle virus, Pepper Veinal Mottle virus, all spread by aphids. Tobacco mosaic and Cucumber mosaic virus are amongst worst.

- ○ **Carthamus tinctorius, SAFFLOWER**

Decaying residues inhibit root growth of wheat.

○ Carum carvi, CARAWAY

Blossoms have been recorded as visited by 55 species of insect: 1 Lepidoptera, 9 species bee, 21 species diptera flies and 24 others.

Deep rooted but difficult to establish, the suggestion has been made to have them follow peas by sowing these together. The caraway germinates once the peas are cleared and the ground harrowed. I suspect this only works in areas with a long enough growing season!

Sustains Swallow-tail Papilio machaon.

○ CEREALS, see also Grasses

Wheat, barley, oats, rice, rye, sweet corn / maize, with their relations the grasses these sustain most of the world's population directly or as animal feed. Although inhibited by weeds, once established these are quite good themselves at inhibiting weeds, and barley and rye are most effective. Thicker stands with closer planting suppress more weeds than thin ones. Mixtures of wheat and rye called 'maslin', oats and barley called 'dredge' were once popular with farmers but hard to sell as difficult to separate the seeds. Either of these or any cereal grown with Legumes such as peas, beans or lupins gives higher yields in total than when cropped alone. In cereal/Legume mixtures the Legumes tend to have their yield reduced relatively more than the cereal. In a trial where cereal and Legume would produce a total of 7 tons grown separately the combination produced 9 tons made up of approximately 6 tons of cereal and 3 tons of Legume. See Grasses to which they are closely related for general associations. Particularly attacked by Corn Aphis / Dolphin / Plant-louse Aphis granaria / avenae.

○ Chenopodium bonus-henricus, GOOD KING HENRY

This little known delicacy has young shoots eaten as asparagus.

Sustains: Nutmeg Hadena trifolii / chenopodii, Orache Trachea atriplicis, Dark Spinach Pelurga comitata (eats flowers and seeds), and Plain Pug Eupithecia subnotata (eats flowers and seeds).

○ Cichorium intybus, CHICORY / SUCCORY

Pretty wild flower and garden form has edible roots and leaves.
Accumulates Iron, Magnesium and some Potassium.
Sustains: Feathered Footman Coscinia striata / grammica, Feathered Brindle Aporophyla australis, and Marbled Clover Heliothis dipsacea / viriplaca (on flowers and seeds).
Damping off and Tomato wilt!

○ Coriandrum sativum, CORIANDER

The seeds are added to bread and baked dishes. The leaf is used in salsas and savoury dishes.
It repels aphids and has been used as a spray against spider mites yet still attracts bees.
Helps germinate anise but hinders seed setting in fennel which itself hinders most other plants.
May carry Clover Yellow Vein virus; yellow mosaic, necrosis and wilting which spreads to most Legumes and also Antirrhinum, Atriplex, Chenopodium, Cucurbita, Gladiolus, Gomphrena, Nicotiana, Nicandra, Papaver, Petunia, Proboscidea, Rubus, Spinacia, Tetragonia and Viola.

○ Corylus avellana, HAZEL / COB / FILBERT

Make excellent wind breaks and beneficial in hedges and pastures for fodder and as fly deterrents.
Plenty of pollen but no nectar as wind pollinated. The cultivated forms such as Cosford cob or Webb's prize cob produce bigger nuts than the wild yet sustain as many forms of wildlife.
Various critters munch their leaves, others leave empty shells of the nuts but the ONLY serious problem is Squirrels. Interestingly if you simply pick the hanging or fallen nuts the percentage with dead or rotten nuts inside the shell is much higher than that of buried nuts- ie. the squirrels only bury good ones. I mulch then after leaf fall rake deeply around the trees recovering many hidden nuts.
Empty shells with a wee hole had kernel eaten by the larvae of the brown Nut Weevil Balininus nucum.
Hazels may get Nut scale which is similar to Peach scale except the base of each is widened just above junction, which spreads to elms, pears, hawthorns and Pyracantha.

The buds can suffer Big Bud where buds swell and distort without opening, all three; leaf-bud, flower bud and catkin bud galls are caused by these acarine gall-mites Eriophyes avellanae / Calycophthora / Phytoptus / Acarus pseudogallarum. These are predated by a midge Arthrocnodax coryligallarum, and a Chalcid Tetrastichus eriophyes and are most vulnerable as the new generation change to new buds in late spring early summer.

Another mite Eriophyes vermiformis may also be found crinkling the leaf.

Hazel sustains 31 Lepidoptera larva.

One of three sustainers Clouded Magpie Abraxas sylvata / ulmata others being Fagus and Ulmus.

Also sustains: Lime Hawkmoth Mimas tiliae, Lobster Moth Stauropus fagi, Iron Prominent Notodonta dromedaries, Coxcomb Prominent Lophopteryx capucina / camelina, Common Lutestring Tethea duplaris, Scarce Vapourer Orgyia recens / gonostigma, Pale Eggar Trichiura crataegii, Broad-bordered Yellow Underwing Lampra fimbriata / fimbria (after hibernation), Beautiful Brocade Hadena contigua, Small Quaker Orthosia cruda / pulverulenta, Sprawler Brachyonycha sphinx / cassinia, Coronet Craniophora ligustri, Green Silver-Lines Bena fagana / prasinana, Nut-tree Tussock Colocasia coryli, Large Emerald Geometra papilionaria, Little Emerald Iodis lactaearia, July Highflyer Hydriomena furcata / elutata / sordidata, Autumnal Moth Oporinia autumnata, November Moth Oporinia dilutata / nebulata, Small White Wave Asthena albulata / candidata, Magpie Abraxas grossulariata, Clouded Border Lomaspilis marginata, Common White Wave Cabera pusaria, Brimstone Moth Opisthograptis luteolata / crataegata, Bordered Beauty Epione repandaria / apiciaria, Buff-Tip Phalera bucephala, Emperor Saturnia pavonia / carpini, Swordgrass Xylena exsoleta, occasionally Blossom Underwing Orthosia miniosa, and Green Hairstreak Callophrys rubi (catkins).

The litter underneath grows the highly poisonous Boletus satanus with a light grey to brown cap, pale blue flesh, most often found on calcerous soils.

The giant edible puffball Calvatia gigantea is often found near hazels and elders.

o **Crambe maritima, SEAKALE**

Decorative and edible UK native, the spring shoots are blanched as crop.

Soft rot Bacterium carotovorum which spreads to carrots, celery and other roots, worse in wet conditions causes stems and other parts to go soft, wet and slimy.

Black Rot, Pseudomonas / Xanthomonas campestris is a bacterial invasion which causes yellowing leaves with blackened veins, cut stems show black dots in a ring, seen most in warm wet years, often attacks cabbage and cauliflower may spread to turnip and swede, introduced on the seed but also soil borne.

Downy mildew Peronospora parasitica can attack seakale much as it does the Brassicas.

May also get Violet Root rot, see carrots Daucus, and worst of all it may get Clubroot, see entry

o **Cucurbits**

All this family are tender, have edible fruits and need warm moist rich conditions.

Most of the following co-lives will have a go at almost any Cucurbit but have been listed under those they visit most.

All are plagued by Red Spider mites in hot dry conditions and Grey mould Botrytis cinerea in cold damp conditions.

These share a common virus Cucumber mosaic, spread by more than 60 aphid species, this invades more than 800 plant species, often first noticed on the fruits which become distorted, mottled and stunted, leaves are smaller, mosaiced, malformed, this may also plague many weeds and crops including pepper, tomato and even blackcurrants, it is known to be spread on the seeds of at least 19 different plant species.

Many other viruses damage Cucurbits world-wide, most are spread by aphids, the name often indicating an alternative host: Bryonia mottle, Clover Yellow Vein virus; yellow mosaic, necrosis and wilting which spreads to most Legumes and also Antirrhinum, Atriplex, Chenopodium, Coriandrum, Gladiolus, Gomphrena, Nicotiana, Nicandra, Papaver, Petunia, Proboscidea, Rubus, Spinacia, Tetragonia and Viola.

Also: Muskmelon vein necrosis, Papaya ringspot-w, Telfairia mosaic (also on seed), Watermelon mosaic, Watermelon mosaic Morocco, Zucchini yellow fleck, Zucchini yellow mosaic (also on seed).

Whiteflies spread: Beet Pseudo-yellows, Cucumber Vein Yellowing, Cucumber Yellows, Lettuce Infectious Yellows, Melon Leaf Curl (also invades Phaseolus beans), Squash Leaf Curl, Watermelon Curly Mottle (also invades Legumes).

Beetles spread: Melon Rugose, Squash mosaic (also on seed), Wild Cucumber mosaic.

Nematodes spread: Tobacco Ringspot (also on seed), Tomato Ringspot.

Thrips spread Tomato Spotted Wilt.

Leaf-hoppers spread Beet Curly Top.

Fungi (on the outside of the zoospores of chytrid fungus Olpidium radicale / cucurbitacearum) spread Cucumber Necrosis, Melon Necrotic Spot (also on seed).

Unknown vectors spread: Cucumber Green Mottle (also on seed), Cucumber Leaf-spot (also on seed), Cucumber Pale Fruit viroid, Ournia Melon virus.

○ **Cucumis melo, MELON**

Accumulates Calcium in leaves.

Melons traditionally like sweet corn / maize, peanuts and sunflowers but not potatoes.

Morning glory is said to stimulate germination of melon seeds, though this may have been confused with a Convolvulus.

These are subject to the usual undercover culprits Aphids, Whitefly, Woodlice, Thrips, and as they're very susceptible to Red Spider mite moist conditions are essential.

Leaf-hoppers Erythroneura pallidifrons bleach leaves (so does sun scorch) so look for the little yellow pests underneath the leaves.

Prone to Neck rot / Canker Bacterium carotovorum where stem emerging from compost goes rotten and whole plant wilts and dies. This is prevented by keeping the neck dry and usually by growing the plant out of a raised mound, even when in a pot.

○ Cucumis sativus, CUCUMBER

Bitter fruits are caused by pollination of indoor varieties, so all male flowers (no wee fruit behind bloom) must be removed. Outdoor or Ridge cucumbers conversely do need pollination.

These do well under sweet corn / maize, or sunflowers in their light shade. They like peas, beans, beet and carrots and Sorghum residues may help them. Dill may aid the plants, and make a trio with sweet corn.

Tomato root exudates shown to inhibit cucumber plants so these should never be planted together. They dislike potatoes mutually and most strong herbs especially sage.

Alfalfa and rye exudates inhibit germination and establishment of cucumbers. Purple nutsedge weeds inhibit growth. Both germination and growth inhibited by yellow starthistle and Pimpinella species.

Stinging nettle tea prevents them getting downy mildew and extracts of garlic and Equisetum control powdery mildew on the cucumbers if used early, and often.

They may attract whitefly off tomatoes.

Stinging nettle tea helps prevent them getting Downy mildew and extracts of garlic and field horsetail control Powdery mildew on cucumbers if used early, and often.

Extremely palatable to Red Spider mite, as these climb upwards some relief can be had by training plants down strings not up.

Cucumbers can be attacked at night by millipedes. Fungus gnats, white legless maggots up to half inch long eat the roots especially in dry conditions. Similar looking Symphalids Scutigerella immaculata may eat the roots at ground level causing corky patches and letting in rots.

Cucumbers are subject to Root Knot eelworm nematode Heterodera radicicol which stunts growth to point of wilt and makes galls on the roots.

Cucumbers suffer Neck rot / Canker Bacterium carotovorum where the stem emerges from the roots, though more of a problem with melons it's worth planting cucumbers on a mound, even in a pot, and keeping the neck dry to prevent this.

If the top dies from dead or decaying damage further up the stem then it is probably Gummy Stem blight Mycosphaerella melonis, this gets in through damage causing a spreading rot, dotted with small black fruiting bodies.

In cold soil cucumbers get Verticillium wilt, in warm soil Fusarium wilt, both result in wilting, yellowing and dessication, the former often shows a stain in the cut stem. Otherwise the symptoms are rather similar to Red Spider mite and may be misdiagnosed either way.

Mildew Erysiphe cichoracearum can cover the younger growths with a powdery coating, this can indicate poor ventilation.

Gummosis Cladosporium cucumerinum is promoted in the cold and wet, it appears on the leaves as small light brown odd shaped spots, these damage growth, but worse are the small soft sunken discoloured, then grey and oozing, spots on the young fruits, which enlarge as they become covered in a thick layer of fungal mycelium and sporulating tissue, then the fruit distorts, cracks and decays.

Blotch Cercospora melonia used to be prevalent but modern varieties are resistant and no longer get the pale water soaked blotches withering the leaves.

Leaf spot / Anthracnose Colletotrichum lagenarium with pale red or green spots can be fatal though better humidity and temperature control and good prompt hygiene removing infected material can halt attacks, this survives on litter and debris.

If the leaves mottle, pucker, wrinkle or distort or have yellow mottling then they have a virus, the commonest being Cucumber Mosaic virus or the harder-to-spot Green Mottle virus which is a transitory light mottle to the leaves as they enlarge, both seriously impede growth and fruiting. Both are spread by aphids Myzus persicae but Green Mottle is also often transmitted on tools etc.

- **Cucurbita maxima, WINTER SQUASHES / PUMPKINS**

These need immense fertility and copious water to get really big. Pick fully ripe with a short length of stem to aid storage.

Exudates suppress germination and growth of many weeds.

They may be healthier with Datura, do not like potatoes and will do well under sweet corn / maize. Purple nutsedge weeds inhibit growth.

- **Cucurbita pepo, MARROW / ZUCCHINNI / COURGETTE / SUMMER SQUASH**

These are the same plant bred to produce different fruits.

Seeds, flowers and fruits edible and during Victorian times some ate the foliage as a spinach (not recommended).

Grows well with sweet corn / maize, peas and beans but avoid potatoes.

Purple nutsedge inhibits growth. Rue was recently proved to be bad for courgettes.

Sustains / suffers Scarce Bordered Straw Heliothis armigera (on immature fruits).

Mildew Erysiphe cichoracearum can cover the younger growths with a powdery coating, this may indicate poor ventilation or water stress.

- ○ **Cynara, GLOBE ARTICHOKE & CARDOON**

The flowers are much loved by humble bees.
Aphids often coat the tender tips and just under the flowerbuds.
These may be attacked by Cassida rubignosa leaf mining beetle larvae and Apion carduorum and A. onopordi stem boring weevils.

- ○ **Cynosurus cristatus, CRESTED DOG'S-TAIL GRASS**

This is eaten by deer and South-down sheep but not readily by Welsh sheep.

- ○ **Dactylis glomerata, COCK'S-FOOT GRASS**

This is eaten by cattle, horses and sheep.
Its germination and growth are both inhibited by exudates from white clover even though this may be donating extra fertility to the soil.
Sustains 23 Lepidoptera larva.

Sole sustainer of 3: Tawny / Marbled Minor Procus latruncula (inside stems), Bordered Gothic Heliophobus anceps / saponariae / reticulata, and Rufous Minor Procus versicolour (inside stems).
One of two sustainers of 2: L-album Wainscot Leucania l-album other being Fescue, and Marbled Minor Procus strigilis (inside stems) other being Agropyron.
One of three sustainers of 2: Shoulder-striped Wainscot Leucania comma others being Rumex species, and Dark Arches Apamea monoglypha / polyodon others being Agropyron repens and Poa annua.
Also sustains: Clouded Brindle Apamea characterea / hepatica, Speckled Wood / Wood Argus Pararge negeria, Wall butterfly Pararge megera, Marbled White Melanargia galathea, Hedge Brown / Gatekeeper Maniola tithonus, Large Skipper Ochlodes venata / sylvanus, Ringlet Aphantopus hyperantus, Drinker Philudoria potatoria, Lunar Yellow Underwing Triphaena orbona / subsequa, Feathered Ear Pachetra sagittigera / leucophaea, Common Wainscott Leucania pallens, Smoky Wainscot Leucania impure, Double Line Mythimna turca, Common Rustic Apamea secalis / oculea / didyma (inside stems), Rosy Minor Procus literosa (inside stems), and Dusky Sallow Eremobia ochroleuca (seeds).

- o **Daucus carota, CARROT, wild and**

cultivated

Do not overfeed or use fresh manure or organic material immediately before carrots as these cause poor flavour and forked roots.

Poor germination often occurs if heavy rain follows sowing.

Heavy soil (carrots prefer a light soil) may be improved for them during the year before sowing incorporating a green manuring of flax and or soya beans.

Carrots stored near apples or pears may acquire a bitter taint.

Germination inhibited by exudates from Jerusalem artichoke, crimson clover, berseem clover, Johnsongrass, hairy vetch, and Pimpinella species, and by leaf leachates from Pluchea lanceolata an Asian weed which also hinders further growth. Yields seriously reduced by Amaranthus palmeri. Wild carrots (in herbage presumably) are said to increase milk yield and flavour of sheep and cows. If left to flower carrots attract hoverflies and beneficial wasps and are recorded as visited by 61 species of insect: 2 butterflies and moths, 8 species bee, 19 species diptera flies and 32 other.

Plagued by Carrot Root fly Psila rosae whose small white larvae tunnel around the carrot roots, two or three generations a year ruin most sowings, overwinters as pupae in soil or as larvae in roots if frost free. This finds carrots by smell, allegedly from up to seven miles away, numerous herbs and strong smelling remedies have been used with some success mostly from onions, leeks and salsify but best preventative is crop rotation, and physical barrier of fleece to stop the fly laying it's eggs by the seedlings, this spreads to celery, parsley, parsnips and also most related umbelliferous weeds such as Cow Parsley

The Aphis Capitophorus eleagni alternates between sea buckthorn and carrots, possiby conflated with the greyish white Carrot aphid SemiAphis dauci found on the foliage causing poor growth and deformed leaves. Another, the greenish Carrot-Willow aphid Cavariella aegopodii does likewise, and also transmits the Carrot Motley Dwarf virus.

The Celery eelworm causes thickening of the leaf bases and weak growth.

The flowerhead of the wild species may be attacked by Dipteron gall-midge Kiefferia / Schizomyia / Asphondylia / Cecidomyia pimpinellae which causes the walls to thicken and the ovary to swell considerably, going greenish yellow to purple or brown, but as carrots are seldom left to flower this does not often get seen in gardens.

Sustains 8 plus Lepidoptera larva: Swallow-tail
Papilio machaon, Ground Lackey Malacosoma
castrensis, Marbled Clover Heliothis dipsacea /
viriplaca (eats flowers and seeds), Red Twin-spot
Carpet Xanthorhoe spadicearia / ferrugata, and
Yellow Belle Aspitates chrearia / citraria.
Also sustains / suffers: Common Flat-Body Moth
Depressaria cicutella, and the seeds by Purple Carrot-
seed Moth D. depressella, both of which are
themselves predated by Odyneri species Solitary
wasps. The carrot flowers and seeds also suffer
Carrot-blossom Moth D. daucella, which may be
lured onto parsnips which they apparently prefer.
Soft Rot, Bacterium carotovorum, makes stored roots
soften and rot away, damage to roots allows this to
get in while growing so only store perfect specimens.
Black Rot, Alternaria radicina, causes black sunken
patches in store.
Violet Root Rot, Helicobasidium purpureum, causes
violet purplish threads to grow over roots, worse in
wet soils with un-rotted organic material, may
spread to many other crops including asparagus,
beet, seakale, clover and alfalfa.
Sclerotinia Rot, caused by S. sclerotiorum, gets in
through damage often near crown, white fluffy mat
rots then tissues mummify and form black sclerotia,
burn all affected roots before it spreads to mangolds,
Dahlias and artichokes which it rots in store and to
potatoes, tomatoes and lettuces which it attacks in
growth.

Carrot Motley Dwarf virus spread by Carrot-Willow Aphis turns the outer leaves red with yellow mottling on inner ones.

○ Digitaria sanguinalis, CRABGRASS

N. American weed, reduces root growth of apple trees.

○ DREDGE

Old companion crop of oats and barley.
In trials with varieties chosen to mature together the mixture gave 2cwt/acre more than when grown separately. Peas and beans were also added in where crop was intended for fodder though then difficult to harvest cleanly.

○ Eruca sativa, ROCKET

Fast growing salad crop, now popular worldwide. A weed in the Middle East, Tribulus terrestris, has leachates that seriously reduce both rockets germination and growth.

- Fagopyrum esculentum, BUCKWHEAT

Calcium and phosphate accumulator and useful green manure.

Secretes plentiful nectar, one of the best hoverfly attractants, and said to make beautiful wax but poor honey.

Dislikes real wheat, and is stimulated in growth by lupins and mustard.

Seed much loved by pheasants and hens.

Sustains / suffers White-line Dart Euoxa tritici / aquilina (young plants).

- Festuca, FESCUES

Grasses, most of these are good at out-competing others and in Kentucky meadows native bluegrass fescues have often squeezed out almost all other plants.

- Festuca arundinacea, TALL FESCUE

Exudates seriously inhibit many grasses, other plants and especially birdsfoot trefoil.

- Festuca duriuscula, HARD FESCUE GRASS

This is eaten readily by most cows, horses and sheep.

- Festuca elatior, MEADOW FESCUE-GRASS

<u>Sole sustainer of</u> Bond's Wainscot Arenostola morrisii / bondii.
<u>One of two sustainers</u> L-album Wainscot Leucania l-album other being Dactylis.
<u>One of three sustainers</u> Cloaked Minor Procus furuncula / bicoloria (in stems) others being Aira caespitosa and Arrhenatherum elatius.
Also sustains: Common Rustic Apamea secalis / oculea / didyma (in stems), and Wall butterfly Pararge megera.

- Festuca ovina, SHEEP'S FESCUE-GRASS

This is eaten readily by cows, horses and sheep.
Sustains 8 Lepidoptera larva.
<u>Sole sustainer of</u> Silver-spotted Skipper Hesperia comma.

Sustains: Marbled White Melanargia galathea, Grayling Satyrus semele, Feathered Footman Coscinia striata / grammica, Northern Rustic Ammogrotis lucernea, Large Heath / Marsh Ringlet butterfly Coenonympha tullia / davus / tiphon, Common Rustic Apamea secalis / oculea / didyma (in stems), and Wall butterfly Pararge megera.

- ### Festuca pratensis MEADOW FESCUE-GRASS

Also liked by cows, horses and sheep.
Sustains: Large Heath / Marsh Ringlet butterfly Coenonympha tullia / davus / tiphon, and Wall butterfly Pararge megera.

- ### Ficus, FIGS

Surprisingly hardy tough plants these are said to do badly near rue.
Avoid the milky sap of figs which can irritate and has been used to treat warts.
Few co-lives visit figs save birds and wasps eating the ripening fruits.

The fruits must be thinned, and most important, all fruits and fruitlets still on outdoor figs in early winter must be removed. This will allow the next set of embryo figs to develop in spring and crop in summer, thin these, and remove all others that appear after. With unbelievable care la Quintayne in France achieved three crops a year forcing potted figs and that was several centuries ago! In UK we have varieties that produce ripe figs without pollination and which are therefore seedless.

On plants on hot walls Red Spider Mite may appear.

o **Foeniculum vulgare, FENNEL**

This just edible herb is often grown more for decoration than use.

Ancient giant fennel, now lost, was the container in which Prometheus carried fire to us humans (the pith burning slowly inside the dried stem).

Italian Finocchio form has edible swollen base and swollen stems refreshing to chew, do not sow early but after mid-summer or it bolts.

Fennel has inhibitory effect on beans, caraway, kohlrabi and tomatoes, dislikes coriander and (as with almost every other plant) hates wormwood.

Fennel is a good host to hoverflies and predatory wasps and may deter aphids from nearby plants.

Sustains: Swallow-tail Papilio machaon, and Mouse Amphipyra tragopogonis.

○ Fragaria, STRAWBERRIES

Shakespeare in Henry V "The strawberry grows underneath the nettle. / And wholesome berries thrive and ripen best / neighboured by fruit of baser quality."

These grow well near the base of peach trees but not under them if shady.

Strawberries love mulches of pine needles, fruits are kept clean with mulches of straw, wheat or barley is fine however avoid oat straw as this may promote root rots.

Brassicas do poorly nearby, any bean especially French does well with them, spinach and lettuce get on and onions grow well in a strawberry bed.

Borage is good amongst strawberries adding to fertility and suppressing weeds.

It's said eating strawberries is good for our teeth, though not with sugar and cream.

The Alpine varieties are good companions bringing in pollinators and predators over their very long flowering season.

Strawberries love mulches of pine needles, and wheat or barley straw but avoid oat straw as this may promote root rots.

When establishing a new bed sow soya beans first then dig these in green to prevent root rots.

Plantains nearby are bad as they are hosts to Myzus ascalonius aphids of both strawberries and shallots.

Not surprisingly THE main co-lives associated with this are Birds. Not much else matters by comparison. Though oddly voles collect up fruits in little piles and eat off all the seeds!

Aphids of several strains especially the yellow Capitophorus fragaefoli are mainly a problem for transmitting virus diseases of which strawberries suffer many.

Leaves reddening and drying up especially in dry weather with a fine web underneath will be Red Spider mite Tetranychus urticae.

Leaves going yellow at the edges, crinkled puckered leaves and dying away could be one of several viruses, or Tarsonemid mite Tarsonemus pallidus, this lives in the centre of the plant, few runners develop, young leaves brown and the problem multiplies especially in warm humid conditions as their lifecycle takes only two weeks or so. The old boys found they could clean their most valuable plants of this mite by plunging them in water at 110 degrees Fahrenheit for twenty minutes then immediately cooling and planting them in a clean bed.

Capsid bugs cause puckered holes in leaves and distorted fruits, as may various Strawberry beetles, a half dozen types of ground living beetles can be found attacking strawberries though only four damage the fruits directly. The Strawberry Seed beetle adult Harpalus rufipes spoils the fruits by eating the seeds, the larvae live on seeds of weeds and then pupate in rough vegetation.

A small black weevil adult, the Strawberry Blossom weevil Anthomonus rubi, often found on raspberries, damages the stem of the fruit causing it to abort, it may attack other soft fruits too leaving a tell tale puncture mark cutting through the stalk.

Another the Strawberry Rhynchites Caenorhinus germanicus, cuts through the leaf and fruit stalks as well causing them to wilt and die, the larvae live in the soil on the roots but allegedly do little harm.

Plants just doing poorly or suddenly wilting and dying should be dug up and examined as it will be vine weevil Otiorhyncus sulcatus, or the similar Strawberry Root weevil O. rugosotriatus, or the Red-legged weevil O. clavipes as found on currants and plums.

As well as weevils the roots are also eaten by leather jackets, wire worms and chafer grubs. This last, Phyllopertha horticola, lives for three years as a white flattish larva with a brown head eating roots of many plants as well as strawberries before pupating into the beetle.

The above ground parts are galled by Leaf and Bud nematode eelworm Aphelencoides / Aphelenchus fragariae and A. ritzemi-bosi, these cause considerable distortions, weakening and stunting even death of the crown.

Similar deterioration may be another eelworm infestation. The Stem eelworm Ditylenchus dipsaci causes the leafstalks to thicken, leaves to become corrugated and flower buds to distort.

Another eelworm Xiphenema diversicaudatum lives on the roots and is important as it carries the Arabis mosaic virus which does far more harm. The same hot water treatment can treat eelworm infested plants as for Tarsonemid mites, see above.

Strawberries are said to be hosts to parasites of the Oriental fruit moth.

The Leaf Button / Strawberry moth Peronea conariana larvae, greenish with yellow head, hatches in late spring eating and webbing together blossom buds and leaves, often living in a web on the underside of leaves.

Sustain 15 other Lepidoptera larvae: Dingy Skipper Erynns tages, Grizzled Skipper Pyrgus malvae / alveolus, Fox Moth Macrothylacia rubi, Kent Black-Arches Nola albula / albulalis, Six-striped Rustic Amathes sexstrigata / umbrosa, Orange Wainscot / Brown-line Bright-eye Leucania conigera, Knotgrass moth Apatele rumicis, Mouse Amphipyra tragopogonis, Beautiful Carpet Mesoleuca albicillata, Yellow Shell Euphyia bilineata, Common Marbled Carpet Dysstroma truncata / russata/ centumnotata, Dark Marbled Carpet Dysstroma citrata / immanata, and Annulet Gnophos obscurata / pullata.

Strawberries also suffer Small / Garden Swift moth Hepialus lupulinus eating their roots.

Strawberries arte very prone to Grey mould Botrytis cinerea in damp conditions which starts as a small grey spot on the flowers or developing fruits and causes complete rot.

Leaf Spot Mycosphaerella fragariae causes small circular spots on leaves that start red, go grey then whitish with dark red edge and may wither the leaves.

Strawberry mildew Spaerotheca macularis produces dark patches on the upper surface and whitish grey patches on the lower leaf surfaces, it overwinters on leaves.

Leaf blotches Gnomonia spp. starts as brown blotches with purplish border surrounded by yellowing, on the leaf stalks may be seen the fungal spores called Black Spheroids.

If the plants weaken become smaller leaved with reddish tints and unproductive this may be Red Core / Lanarkshire disease Phytophthora fragariae, the sure sign is the roots are withered and blackened except for a red core.

Strawberry Crinkle virus causes loss of vigour and crinkled leaves, spread by creamy white Strawberry aphid Chaetosiphon fragaefolii which fly from plant to plant in early summer.

Strawberry Yellow Edge virus is another that reduces vigour, and causes a yellow edge to the leaves, also spread by aphid C. fragaefolii.

The Arabis mosaic virus mentioned above is spread by the eelworm Xiphenema diversicaudatum living on the roots and the virus causes the leaves to blotch, mottle and the veins to thicken.

A host of other viruses are sadly also possible.

○ Glycine max, SOYA beans

These must have their mycorrhizal fungal partner or grow badly.

Too tender for most European gardeners, newer varieties may just crop here.

An acre in the USA yields above 15cwt of beans, about 13cwt dried giving 500-600lb of crude protein and containing 200-250lb oil and about 500lb carbohydrate.

The green parts contain 0.25-0.3% Phosphorus and 1.3% Calcium.

The plants are hosts to Trichogramma wasps and have been used to deter cinchworms, chinchbugs, corn earworms, corn borers and Japanese beetles.

Soya beans must have their right mycorrhizal fungal partners to thrive.

Soya bean residues hinder germination of corn / maize until well decayed.

Soya is itself reduced in germination and growth by couch grass. Germination inhibited by Palmer amaranth, other weeds: morning glory, velvetleaf, fat hen, redroot pigweed and yellow foxtail, seriously reduce growth and seed production.

They can carry Clover Yellow Vein virus; yellow mosaic, necrosis and wilting which spreads to most other Legumes: and also Antirrhinum, Atriplex, Chenopodium, Coriandrum, Cucurbita, Gladiolus, Gomphrena, Nicotiana, Nicandra, Papaver, Petunia, Proboscidea, Rubus, Spinacia, Tetragonia and Viola.

They also carry Soybean mosaic virus; blistering, leaf cupping, necrosis, wilting and death, also seriously affects beans.

As bad is Bean Curly Dwarf mosaic; mosaic, stunting and rugosity, this also infects other Phaseolus species, pea, chickpea, lentil, broad bean, mung bean and Leguminous weeds.

Bean Southern mosaic; green mosaic with rugocity also infects beans, cowpeas, peas and other Legumes. Thrips tabaci and Frankliniella occidentalis spread Tobacco Streak virus / Bean Red Node; red nodes, necrosis and red spots, also seed borne this also spreads to alfalfa, chickpea, fenugreek, Datura, sweet clover, Nicotiana, beans and many plants.

Whiteflies Bemesia spp. transmits Euphorbia mosaic; necrotic lesions and distortion, this also infects lentils and other Legumes.

o **GRASSES**

Closely related plants to agricultural cereals and rice, sugar cane and maize. Tough wearing grasses like lime, the fine leaved 'bowling green' grasses like acid soil. The tough ones make better swards for almost all purposes except bowling greens.

Clover helps grass immensely, so cut high to spare it. Daisies indicate grass is being cut too close, and probably short of lime.

The best fertiliser to stimulate without overfeeding is well diluted urine, use this natural renewable resource and make a bonus water saving from less flushing.

Grasses may inhibit each other, their frost killed leaves inhibit re-growth and exudates of dead leaves inhibit germination of other species as well as the donor.

Many grasses are reluctant hosts to parasitic plants; Yellow Rattle Rhinanthus crista-galli, Lousewort Pedicularis and Eyebright Euphrasia officinalis.

All aerial parts of most grasses galled by nematode eelworm Tylenchus dipsaci, this causes considerable distortions, weakening and stunting.

Very rarely the Hessian fly, a minute yellowish grub, may cause poor growth as these sap the base of the leaves.

Many grasses are alternate hosts for such as Aphis granaria / avenae Corn aphid / Dolphin, of cereals, Frit Fly Oscinis frit and the devastating Ergot of rye Claviceps purpurea.

Dressings of maize flour stimulate growth in grass and suppress annual weeds, clover and dandelions. Milk has a similar beneficial effect when applied diluted.

In orchards grass will inhibit growth especially under pears however this is of use once the trees are established as excessive tree growth reduces fruiting. The competition of grass is particularly bad for newly planted trees and shrubs especially if regularly cut, the soil should be mulched or weeded for a radius of at least the height of the plant.

Timothy grasses use their pollen to prevent nearby plants setting viable seed; just ten grains of their pollen on the stigma of other plants can prevent them setting viable seed!

Sustain / suffer over 25 Lepidoptera larvae.

Sustain: White-speck Wainscot Leucania unipuncta, Delicate Wainscot Leucania vitellina, Cosmopolitan Leucania loreyi, Union Rusttic Apamea pabulatricula / connexa, Large Nutmeg Apamea infesta / anceps / sordida, Smoky Wainscot Leucania impura, Southern Wainscot Leucania straminea, Common Wainscot Leucania pallens, Shoulder-Knot Apamea basilinea, White Ear / Common Rustic Apamea didyma, Middle-Barred Minor Miana / Procus fascinuncula / fasciuncula, Anomalous Stilbia anomala, Hay Moth / Pale Mottled Willow Caradrina quadripunctata, Dark Swordgrass Agrotis suffusa / ipsilon, Heart and Dart Agrotis exclamationis, Double Dart Noctua / Graphiphora augur, Clouded Brindle Xylophasia rurea, Dark Arches Xylophasia monoglypha (on roots), Feathered Gothic Neuronia / Pachetra popularis (on roots), and Ear Moth Hydraecia nictitans (on roots).

Suffers: Silver Gamma / Y moth Plusia gamma, Antler / Grass Moth Cerapteryx / Charaeus graminis, Belted Beauty Nyssia zonaria, and Great Yellow Underwing moth Noctua / Tryphaena pronuba (roots and leaves).

Cereals and grasses sustain serious damage to roots from Small / Garden Swift moth Hepialus lupulinus which also attacks parsnip, lettuce, potato, celery, strawberry and beans.

Damping off is a fungal attack with patches of grass dying back after yellowing or reddening and wilting, most prevalent in damp humid conditions, often where growth is poor due to low light or poor soil conditions.

In warmer weather especially in late summer Fusarium Patch or Snow mould can cause yellowish brownish burnt out holes, sometimes huge, dying going slimy and becoming covered in whitish or pinkish cotton.

If however there is a sticky redness, the grass looks bleached but does not waste away then it could be Corticium or Red Thread. A lens will reveal red spiky outgrowths from the tips.

Very rarely there may be little white mycelia showing on the burnt out spots which are more browny yellowish than bleached and this shows Dollar Spot.

Little black dots at the base of the stems indicates an Ophiobolus attack.

A general dirty yellowishness and a fine powdery coating will be a Mildew attack.

Fairy Ring champignon fungus Marasmius oreades, edible, buff tan cap with deeply cut and wide spaced whitish gills, smells of burnt almonds, this creates green rings, these are formed as the fungus moves outwards from its original spot leaving enriched soil for the grass.

Likewise Blewits Lepista saeva / Tricholoma saevum / bicolor / personatum grow in grasses in rings, they have buff tan caps with brown gills and an ink stained stem (stipe), they are edible, tasty and even remain edible once frosted, but must always be cooked.

The edible Horse mushroom Agaricus / Psalliota arvensis has a white cap, greyish gills and a slight scent of aniseed, if scratched the flesh turns yellow, also found in spruce forests (the inedible and similar Yellow stainer Agaricus / Psalliota xanthodermus / xanthoderma is yellow at the base of the stipe and smells of carbolic).

The best known of all edible mushrooms is the Field mushroom Agaricus / Psalliota campestris, white cap with pink gills, this is found in damp meadows especially round the edges in the lee of hedges.

Hygrophorus conicus / conica, inedible, has a reddish orange or yellow conical cap, yellowish gills, tastes bitter, turns black with age or when dried and often appears in fields and meadows after rain.

Likewise Stropharia coronilla appears after rains, it has a yellowish white to tan ochre cap with chocolate brown gills and spores and an unusually short stipe, it is inedible.

St George's mushroom Calocybe / Tricholoma gambosa / gambosum / georgii appears in spring on the sunny edges of woods hiding in grassy clumps, it is edible and tasty, has a fleshy pale cap with narrow crowded gills, and white spores, it has a marked floury taste and smell.

○ GREEN MANURES

Plants sown to produce fertility rather than for a direct crop. These are usually sown when the land is not needed and act as cover crops preventing soil erosion and leaching.

A green manure may be incorporated by digging in, by composting in situ under an opaque sheet, or by stripping off and composting elsewhere before returning.

Hungarian Grazing rye / perennial ryegrass, Lolium perenne, produces masses of fibrous top growth. Tares, vetches, clovers, lupins and other Legumes are often used to fix Nitrogen. Others like mustard produce masses of fine roots.

I prefer utilising less troublesome plants than the above offerings which come from farming where they have ploughs to assist. I find Claytonia perfoliata, Valerianella and Limnanthes douglassi to be the most useful for winter, with spinach, borage, buckwheat and Phacelia for summer.

○ Helianthus annuas, SUNFLOWER

Edible seeds, much beloved by wild birds and hens, these have been roasted for coffee.

The flowers are very good for bees, lacewings and predatory wasps.

The foliage is good for cows and sheep, and the stems are rich in potash.

Hungry feeders these inhibit many plants especially oats, potatoes, runner beans and grass.

They're inhibited from germinating themselves by grass and by Datura species. Yields seriously reduced by N. American weeds Amaranthus palmeri and Johnson grass.

Cucumbers and other Cucurbits will grow (if planted not sown) underneath and given enough fertility and water.

Rust Puccinia helianthi causes brown powdery mounds on leaves and stems, the leaves dry and wither, the seeds may become infected.

○ Helianthus tuberosus, JERUSALEM ARTICHOKE

Edible if not palatable perennial standby crop, closely related and much resemble sunflowers, useful for when the potatoes fail, not much loved as these tubers give you wind.

These make a quickly established tall screen during summer months though bare in winter.

If you need to get rid of these graze geese for a month or two, seriously this has worked, and profitably.

These can grow with sweet corn / maize when sufficient richness and moisture are available.

The variety Fuseau suppresses ground elder and Equisetum.

Leaf extracts seriously inhibit germination of carrot, radish, pea, Inula and Acer.

Can be attacked by fungus Sclerotinia sclerotiorum which causes white fluffy growths on stem and tubers with hard brownish black sclerotia forming on and in the stems and tubers, worst in wet acid soils.

- ## Holcus lanatus, MEADOW SOFT GRASS / YORKSHIRE FOG

This grass is generally disliked by cows, sheep and horses both fresh and as hay.

Host to Brassica Clubroot disease and Stem eelworm Tylenchus devastatrix.

One of two sustainers Lunar Underwing Omphaloscelis lunosa other being Poa.

Also sustains: Antler Cerapteryx graminis, Small Skipper Thymelicus sylvestris / linea / thaumus, and Large Skipper Ochlodes venata / sylvanus.

- Holcus mollis, CREEPING SOFT-GRASS

Sustains: Large Skipper Ochlodes venata / sylvanus, and Common Rustic Apamea secalis / oculea / didyma (in stems).

- Hordeum distichon / vulgare, BARLEY

Cereal grown for animal feed, and beer after malting. Ashes contain 4% potash, 17% soda, 3.4% lime, 10% magnesia, 2% Iron oxide, negligible Manganese oxide, 41% phosphoric acid, 0.3% sulphuric acid, 22% silica and a little chlorine.

In a trial germination was reduced by soil organism Gliocladium roseum, this was counteracted by Azotobacter chroococcum but ONLY when this was grown in a nitrate free medium. In other words seeds not only do not need soluble fertilisers but using them will hinder success.

Used to be grown as mixed crop with oats and peas or beans.

It resists weeds more effectively than wheat inhibiting the germination of grasses and clovers and may inhibit germination and seedling growth of alfalfa, wheat and radish.

Purple nutsedge inhibits its growth. Salvia syriaca drastically reduces germination, growth and yield.

The inflorescence stalk is attacked by Dipteron chloropid Chlorops taeniopus Gout fly or Ribbon-footed corn-fly which lays eggs on the leaves or stalks, the larvae get into the shoots which thicken and form cigar shaped galls, the flower fails and the fly after hatching moves to an alternate host, often couch grass.

One of three sustainers Flounced Rustic Luperina testacea (on roots) others being Avena and Triticum. Also sustains: Rosy Minor Procus literosa (in stems), Rosy Rustic Hydraecia micacea (in stems), and Brighton Wainscot Oria musculosa (in stems).

o Hordeum murinum, WILD BARLEY

Tribulus terrestris, a weed of Middle East, has leachates that seriously reduce its germination and growth.

o Humulus lupulus, HOP

Very vigorous dioecious herbaceous climbers, weak growing dwarfer forms becoming available.
The shoots are edible but bitter, change the water thrice.
Pestered by wireworms which may be lured onto trap planting of potatoes.

Female plant 'flowers' are the hops (despite the dusty resin being termed pollen which it is manifestly not). The male plants are discouraged on continent as seeds in the hops for brewing hinder the bottom fermenting yeasts used in lagers but not top fermenting yeasts used in good old British beer.

Host to Stem eelworm Tylenchus devastatrix.

Hops suffer hosts of aphids, which feed Stethoras ladybirds which also eat whiteflies.

Sustains 16 Lepidoptera larva.

<u>Sole sustainer of</u> Buttoned Snout Hypena rostralis.

<u>One of two sustainers of 3</u>: Snout Hypena proboscidalis other being Urtica dioica, Dark Spectacle Abrostola triplasia / trigemina other being Urtica dioica, and Peacock Nymphalis / Inachis io other also being Urtica dioica.

<u>One of three sustainers of 2</u>: Currant Pug Eupithecia assimilata others being Ribes species, and Red Admiral Vanessa atalanta others being Parietaria and Urtica dioica.

Also sustains: Comma Polygonia c-album Pale Tussock Dasychira pudibunda, Cinnabar Callimorpha jacobaea, Clouded Drab Orthosia incerta / instabilis, Twin-Spotted Quaker Orthosia munda, Knotgrass moth Apatele rumicis, Mottled Rustic Caradrina morpheus, Rosy Rustic Hydraecia micacea, and occasionally Privet Hawkmoth Sphinx ligustri.

○ Juglans regia, ENGLISH WALNUT

These become very big trees and take a long time to fruit, the male and female flowers often not out at same time are wind pollinated.

Be warned handling walnut leaves and especially the shucks of the fruits as these soften, will stain your skin and clothes indelibly.

Varro remarked on the sterility of land near walnuts, the American species are worse exuding juglone which has proven hostile to most plants.

Often trees carry huge quantities of yellow lichens unseen on the upper side of branches.

Some nuts are dead inside but this is as often from the year being too dry as from any disease.

Squirrels do their usual.

Blister Mite are leaf blisters caused when leaf-blade galled by acarine gall-mite Eriophyes tristriatus typicus / Phytoptus / Erineum juglandinum / Phyllerium juglandis, making a shiny bulge on top surface but infestation is underneath where mites live in hollow filled with downy hairs.

Surprisingly you may find a familiar looking maggot in your walnut as rather rarely these are attacked by the same Codling Moth as haunts apples.

Blotches on the leaves made of spotty bits forming a whole not just one plain blotch is likely Bacterial Blight Xanthomonas juglandis which will cause twigs to die back from black streaks on the shoots, and spots on leaves and fruits, the fruits become rotted, shell-less and soggy inside.

Leaf Blotch or Leaf Spot fungus Marssonina juglandis / Gnomonia leptostyla causes yellowish brown patches greyish on the underside of the leaves going brown with spots also appearing on the shuck or fruit covering.

The trunks, stumps and large branches, dead and alive, support a semi-circular bracket fungus Polyporus / Polyporellus squamosus, brown scales with white edible flesh smelling of cucumber, this grows quickly, can reach many pounds in weight but harms trees causing the wood to decay with timber White rot, spreads to beech, horse chestnut, lime, poplar and willow.

○ **Lactuca sativa, LETTUCE**

Edible though it contains 'opiates' in sap when near flowering causing intense bitterness, must be grown fast to be succulent.

Lettuce has been shown to take up natural antibiotics from the soil.

If it's hot sow lettuce in shade as it will not germinate above 65 degrees F.

Does best amongst cucumbers, carrots, radish and strawberries and may not prosper near broccoli.

Croton bonplandianum exudates seriously reduce germination as does rue, rye, Miscanthus, Palmer amaranth and small everlasting Antennaria.

Growth inhibited by Asian weeds, Purple nutsedge, Leersia hexandra, Bothriochloa pertusa and Borreria articularis.

Most Brassicas, Yellow starthistle, Cassia sophera, Crotolaria pallida, Pimpinella species Sasa cernua, Xanthium strumarium, tomato and tobacco root exudates, all inhibit germination and suppress growth of lettuce.

Lettuce suffer from a host of different aphids, a half dozen on the leaves early in the season particularly Macrosiphum solani, greenish, often found on underside of leaves. Then later, even worse, Lettuce Root aphids Pemphigus bursarius which stunt growth, however growing chervil nearby may help protect them. The root aphid over-winters as eggs on poplar trees especially Populus nigra later moving on to the leaf stalks there forming galls which split in midsummer when the aphids move back onto lettuce. (Anthocorid bugs destroy these galls and reduce the pest numbers and these apparently 'live' on chervil.) Old time gardeners used a solution made from elderberry leaves boiled in soft soap to drench the roots and claimed this killed the root aphids.

The Root Knot eelworm Heterodera marioni can cause the roots to get galls the size of dots or as big as plums, this spreads to tomatoes, cucumbers and beans.

Symphalids Scutigerella immaculata may eat the roots at ground level causing corky patches and letting in rots.

Sustains: Grey Chi moth Antitype chi, Shark Cucullia umbratica, Broad-barred White Hadena serena (eats flowers and seeds), and Small Ranunculus Hadena dysodea / chrysozona (eats flowers and seeds).

Suffers: Small / Garden Swift moth Hepialus lupulinus and both roots and leaves attacked by fat, black striped larvae of Great Yellow Underwing moth Noctua / Tryphaena pronuba.

Downy mildew Bremia lactucae turns leaves yellowish brown and stunts the plants while Grey Mould Botrytis cinerea gets in through wounds, turns the leaves and then whole plant grey and rotten.

Ring spot Marssonina panattoniana prevalent in cold wet conditions; brown patches on underside of leaf ribs appear first then brown spots on outer leaves which fall out after turning whitish to leave white margined holes, then rot moves into centre and often kills plant, spread on debris.

Lettuce Mosaic virus is transmitted by aphids and on the seed, the leaves mottle while the veins go transparent and growth is stunted, also invades more than twenty genera in ten families.

Lettuce Infectious Yellow virus, spread by whiteflies, also invades Cucurbits.

Turnip mosaic virus, spread by aphids, also invades most cruciferous plants.

Bidens Mottle virus, spread by aphids, also invades lettuce and endive and does serious damage in Florida.

Lettuce Big Vein virus, spread by soil borne fungus Olpidium Brassicae on surface of zoospores.

Beet Western Yellows virus, spread by aphids, also invades many other plants as does Lettuce Necrotic Yellows virus, also spread by aphids.

Lettuce Mottle virus, spread by aphid Hyperomzus lactucae.

Cucumber mosaic virus, spread by more than 60 aphid species, invades more than 800 plant species. Can also be infected by virus Broad Bean Wilt; yellow mosaic and distortion this also infects spinach, pea, broad bean and other Legumes.

○ LEGUMES

The largest family of plants to fix Nitrogen from the air (several others may but these are mostly tropical). They achieve this with nodules on their roots which harbour microbes which do the fixation in return for nutrients from the plant.

Trees such as Laburnum, Judas tree, and Caragana, shrubs such as brooms and tree lupins are Leguminous as well as the clovers, peas, beans and lupins we usually think of. All of them benefit other plants by supplying Nitrogen as their root hairs and associated micro-organisms decompose.

The beans should be grown more as they enrich the soil and if not eaten fresh can be easily dried for storage.

In general annual Legumes do well mutually with carrots, Brassicas and beets and help cucumbers. Legumes may also be grown with borage, potatoes, squashes, strawberries and tomatoes. They are happy with sweet corn and cereals.

Although in general Legumes hate onions and their family they may aid leeks but only when in small proportion and similarly with celeriac.

Most Legumes especially clovers are an alternate host for Clover Yellow Vein virus, spread by aphids, which attacks many plants including Cucurbits and especially squash.

They host Muskmelon Vein Necrosis virus spread by aphids.

Legumes can also be infected by Watermelon Curly Mottle virus spread by whiteflies.

o Linum usitatissimum, FLAX

As a field crop (for seed for oil) or as green manure it's very beautiful in flower, and very attractive to a host of insects.

It leaves a very tough fibrous haulm which makes excellent compost, though slowly.

Ashes contain 26% potash, 1.5% soda, 26% lime, 0.2% magnesia, 4% iron oxide, negligible manganese oxide, 40% phosphoric acid, 1% sulphuric acid, 1% silica and 1% chlorine.

Grown as a green manure or intercrop it benefits carrots and potatoes. Should not follow Brassicas. Germination and growth suppressed by Datura and Euphorbia species.

- ## Lolium multiflorum, ITALIAN RYEGRASS

Germination inhibited by Lantana camara, Miscanthus, crimson clover, hairy vetch, Pimpinella and Linaria vulgaris.
The nectar is only accessible to long lipped bees whilst other insects are excluded.
The roots are attacked by Coleopteran weevils Gymnetron linariae / collinum which larvae live in small spherical galls, G. hispidum causes elongated galls on the stems.
The shoots are galled by hymenopteran gall-wasp Aulacidea hieracii / Aylax / sabaudi / graminis / Cynips which over-winter in the gall.

- ## Lolium perenne, PERENNIAL RYEGRASS, HUNGARIAN GRAZING RYE

Superb deep rooter, good cover crop and green manure, but hard to kill off.
provides masses of fibrous material.
Sheep prefer it young and dislike it mature.
Germination inhibited by exudates from white clover and Erica australis.
Germination and growth inhibited by yellow starthistle.
Lantana camara inhibits root growth.

Sustains: Wall butterfly Pararge megera, Hedge Brown / Gatekeeper Maniola tithonus, and Meadow Brown Maniola jurtina / janina.

o Lolium temulentum, DARNEL

Although a grass this has poisonous seeds, these recorded roasted to give off an early form of riot control gas.
Sustains Dusky Sallow Eremobia ochroleuca (seeds).

o Lycopersicon esculentum, TOMATOES

Closely related to potatoes, tobacco, peppers and aubergines so ideally these all should be kept apart, both physically and in rotation.
Some Biodynamic growers grow them in the same place for years without rotation feeding them compost made from their own leaves.
Interestingly they have been shown to take up antibiotics from the soil. Tomatoes can be protected from Botrytis by coating them with yeasts, these may occur naturally when honeydew from aphid infestations drips onto them, an interesting concept in crop protection.

Tomato root exudates inhibit couch grass, and also cucumber plants so these should never be planted together. Same or other exudates from tomato leaves suppress radish, lettuce, Sorghum, Perilla, and Brassica campestris, and volatile exudates hinder grapevines and maize. Tomatoes nearby may inhibit apricot seedlings.

A strange allegedly effective combination is having tomatoes protecting roses from blackspot, and they may be 'protective' to gooseberries (though against what was not stipulated, the mildew or sawfly?). Germination of tomatoes is inhibited by Pimpinella species Palmer amaranth and Digera alternifolia, an Asian weed. Growth is inhibited by other Asian weeds Bothriochloa pertusa, Pluchea lanceolata and Purple nutsedge. Rue is thought to prevent tomato seeds from germinating and alfalfa exudates to reduce growth. Like most plants tomatoes loathe fennel and wormwood and dislike all the Brassica family especially kohlrabi. However they're reputed to aid early cabbage which seems unlikely as their growing seasons hardly touch.

Tomatoes get on well with basil, Alliums, marigolds and nasturtiums, and keep for longer if grown near nettles (stinging I presume). Some varieties agree some disagree with parsley. Tomatoes do particularly well with asparagus.

Bits of the leaf do repel flea beetles.

Tomato leaf spray has been used against asparagus beetles and asparagus roots kill Trichodorus, a nematode that attacks tomatoes.

Including Tagetes in crop rotations reduces nematode populations by 85%. Tagetes erecta grown with tomatoes protects them from soil fungal disease Alternaria solani.

Interestingly they have been shown to take up antibiotics from the soil. Tomatoes can be protected from Botrytis by coating them with certain yeasts, these may occur naturally when honeydew from aphid infestations drips onto them, an interesting concept in crop protection.

In the greenhouse White fly, Thrips, Leaf-hoppers, Red Spider mite and Mealy bug are their usual troublesome.

Spring tails cause the plants to wilt and can be found on the roots as tiny whitish purplish critters which hop about but are easily eliminated with soft soap. Symphalids Scutigerella immaculata may eat the roots at ground level causing corky patches and letting in rots. Both these last are commonest in plants raised under glass.

The roots are attacked by nematodes / eelworms Heterodera spp. especially H. marioni known to attack over 800 different plants, these cause gall swellings on roots, the males leave to search for females, these remain in the old galls, swell and turn into a cyst of up to five hundred eggs, these develop into juveniles within the cyst and later leave, up to a year or more later, the roots may get woody galls the size of dots or as big as plums.

Most Potato eelworms especially Heterodera schachtii also attack tomatoes, plants will wilt during day and small white cysts will be found on roots.
Suffer: Beautiful Brocade Hadena contigua, and Brown Brocade / Bright-line Brown Eye Diataraxia oleracea, and especially the Tomato moth Polia oleracea caterpillar, greenish to reddy brown or yellow, up to two inches long, eats the leaves underside first then finishes whole lot, it eats at night and if disturbed drops, onto waiting sheets of newspaper if you're foresighted.
Bacterial canker Corynebacterium michiganense may affect the leaves which brown on one side only of the leaf stalk which has yellow brown streaking inside, the fruit may have spotting and streaking from the stalk end. The bacteria can survive several years on strings, canes and debris and beware 'suspicious source' seed as this may be infected.
Botrytis Stem rot causes grey sunken areas on stem usually in badly made pruning wounds.
Seedlings suffer Damping Off caused by many different fungi, Phytophthora cryptoga, P. parasitica, Corticum solani and others, clean compost, clean water, dryish bright conditions and good ventilation help prevent the wilting and dying.
Once seedlings get larger they then may suffer Foot Rot from similar fungi, however plants may grow away from these if not killed and where the stem can reroot above the lesion.

Root rot Colletotrichum atramentarium attacks later stages of plant including mature, most often mid to late summer, roots turn brown not healthy white, symptoms are wilting of older leaves during day but recovering at night.

Tomato canker / Stem-rot fungus Didymella lycopersici is a root disease, fruit may be infected, dark brown lesions occur on stem base at or below soil level, these can be seen to have tiny black spores, pinkish tendrils extend and may infect other tissues especially through wounds, leaves may get grey lesions in damp conditions. In bad cases large plants suddenly wilt, you find a black ulcer or canker rotting the stem base, it's carried through winter on debris, strings and supports.

Wilt or Sleepy Disease is similar caused by Verticillium albo-atrum, affected plants can be saved by earthing up at base, syringing foliage but keeping soil dryish, and keeping plants warmer (above 77° F), just because it is temperature dependent so Verticillium is not often seen in summer.

Fusarium wilt is opposite, occurs most often in hot periods.

Leaf Mould / Rust, Cladosporium fulvum, causes yellowish blotches on top of leaves with purplish underneath, leaves become brown and brittle, this is prevalent under cover and in warm humid conditions especially where plants are over-crowded, spreads by spores so remove all debris and litter after crop finished, it weakens plants and reduces crops but fruits otherwise unaffected.

Beware that tomatoes may harbor Wart disease which attacks the roots, see potatoes.

Tomatoes, particularly if outdoors, share Potato Late Blight Phytophthora infestans with potatoes with similar dire results.

Tomatoes are also susceptible to Early Blight Alternaria solani which looks much the same at first with black or brownish spots on the leaves and stems. However these are a bit more angular in shape and on the stems the spots are sunken and not streaked. On the fruits Late blight causes random rotten spots, Early Blight causes the fruit to rot mostly at the flower end this becoming covered with a black mat of mycelium.

Tomatoes are invaded by over 40 viruses worldwide. Raspberries share Tomato Black Ring virus.

Tobacco Mosaic virus causes serious losses, leaves mottle dark green and young growth is distorted, then as fruiting starts brown streaks appear on stems which become brittle. Often infection starts with a smoker who carries it in on their hands or their tobacco, commercial growers stopped most attacks when they banned smokers from their greenhouses, also transmitted on pruning equipment.

Tomato mosaic virus, spread by aphids, on tools, in soil and on seed, may reduce yields by a quarter, also invades tobacco and datura.

Cucumber mosaic virus is also found invading tomatoes and peppers and aubergines.

Tomato Ringspot virus, spread by nematodes, also invades Cucurbits and hundreds of other plants both woody and herbaceous.
Tomato Spotted Wilt virus, spread by thrips, also invades Cucurbits.
Beet Curly Top virus is spread by leaf-hoppers and also invades Cucurbits and many other plants.
In warmer climates the sweet potato whitefly Bemisia tabaci spreads Tomato Yellow Leaf Curl virus, Tomato Leaf Curl virus, Tobacco Leaf Curl virus, Chino del tomate virus, Tomato Yellow Dwarf virus and Tomato Golden mosaic virus.
Tobacco Etch virus and Vein Banding mosaic virus spread by aphids also invade tomatoes.

o ## Malus, APPLE

Grown everywhere so very many associated co-lives, and therefore many parasites and predators of those as well.
Old trees and especially Cooking / Culinary varieties will often derive great benefit from wood ashes.
Be careful to store only perfect fruit and to keep these away from strong herbs, potatoes and carrots which will taint them. Separate late from early ripeners and use dried nettles to help preserve and ripen them.
Apples give off ethylene gas as they ripen, this may inhibit plant growth and cause premature maturation in other flowers and fruits.

Said that in ripe fruit the round seeds will be most like parent and flat seeds more like crab.

Alliums under the trees, especially chives and garlic, discourage fungal diseases.

Apples are said to benefit from nasturtiums underneath which drive away the Woolly Aphis.

Penstemons keep the Sawflies away.

Wormwood and crabgrass seriously depress root growth.

Grass and weeds inhibit growth, especially unwelcome during the early years, keep these cleared all round for at least the trees height by using mulches. Older trees may be grassed around, include clovers for fertility and alfalfa / Lucerne in sward to bring nutrients up from deep down.

Apple trees said to cause potatoes nearby to be prone to Blight.

June Drop is not a disease or a pest attack but looks disastrous; around midsummer depending on the tree's assessment of it's cropping ability it drops a large number of fruitlets leaving fewer to swell and ripen.

Bitter Pit is another not very common problem sometimes found with old trees on worked out soils, especially on acid soils. Basically a shortage of water causes lots of small brown spots to appear throughout the flesh especially just under the skin. Mulches improving soil moisture and enhancing the microlife population reduce this physiological condition; it's not a pest or disease as it does not spread.

Watery Core or Glassiness of the fruit is another physiological disorder where the core seems to be waterlogged. It's worst in young, over fertilised trees in high temperatures with extremes of water stress, I find Charles Ross particularly prone.

Wasps rely on birds to start the holes for them and our friends the Blue tits and Blackbirds are common culprits pecking holes in ripening fruits.

Very corky scarred or distorted leaves and fruits may be showing earlier damage from Apple Capsid Plesiocoris rugicollis, adult quarter inch long and green, attacks making small punctures in the leaves and shoots (brown or black marks), then moves onto the fruits where their punctures cause corky patches that expand with the fruit making them unsightly and prone to other problems. They hatch in spring from eggs buried under the bark, moult five times getting bigger and eventually grow wings and mate. Apple Suckers Psylla mali look much like aphids though under a lens are red eyed, yellow green with green wings, they cause similar problems to aphids with distorted leaves and failed flower buds, damage is lessened as only one batch a year, from overwintering eggs.

In hot dry conditions Fruit Tree Red Spider mites, Panonychnus uni can cause their usual trouble browning leaves and bringing on autumn colouring early in summer, usually predated by the Capsid bug Anthocoris nemorum.

Bryobia mites Bryobia rubrioculus are dependent on apple and pear trees with no alternate host, they suck sap breed rapidly and they and their damage much resemble red spider mite except they are not hairy and have longer front legs.

Chafer beetle adults of Melolantha melolantha and Phyllopertha horticola eat the leaves and small fruitlets, while their larvae eat the roots.

Bark beetles Anisandrus dispar, bore into the wood all the way to the middle, usually of already weakened specimens which it further degrades, though thought to get most of it's sustenance not from the chewed up wood but from fungi on the tunnel walls.

Several weevils attack parts of apple trees though seldom badly, in particular Leaf weevil Phyllobious oblongus and P. piri adults may graze and thus harm seedling trees though their larvae eat the roots of grasses.

The Apple Fruit Rhynchites weevil R. aquatus is brownish red, attacks the fruits a fortnight after petal fall, damage as if a biro pen has been pushed hundreds of times into the flesh.

The Apple Twig Cutter weevil Rhynchites caeruleus, has a dark blue adult, rather beautiful and well named for the larvae does just that to the ends of twigs which fall off in summer, the adults emerge and over-winter to eat leaves and bark before laying their eggs from late spring.

The yellowish Apple Blossom weevil, Anthonomus pomorum, causes flower buds to brown and stay shut, the 'cap' can be lifted off to show the grub within and prove it's not frost damage.

The white Apple Bud weevil, Anthonomas cinctus, often attacks pears worse causing dead buds and shoot tip damage.

Leaf-hoppers Erythroneura alneti and Typhocyba froggatti are greenish jumpers that suck the sap as adults and also as nymphs causing leaves to wither or colour early.

Aphids are often evident and in at least 8 varieties. The Green apple aphid Aphis pomi, the Oak apple aphid Rhodslosiphum invertum and the Rosy apple aphid Sappapthis mali are commonest, these usually do modest harm, though heavy infestations cause leaf curling and distortion, plus their honeydew causes sooty moulds.

Branches, roots and stems are attacked by Homopteran aphid Eriosoma lanigerum / mali / Schizoneura / Aphis lanigera the dreaded American Woolly aphid or American blight. Swellings and cankers form with woolly fluffy covering protecting these aphids spread aerially on wind buoyed up by the fluff. Woolly Aphis is remarkably common in old untended overgrown orchards and rare in open well pruned ones. A North American wasp Aphelinus mali has been introduced to Europe and may now help to control Woolly Aphis which has not proved palatable to most local fauna. Growing trailing nasturtiums in profusion under the trees is reputed to drive Woolly Aphis away but takes several years. Scale insects often found on old trees and in overgrown orchards and particularly on wall specimens. Mussel Scale, Mytilococcus / Lepidosaphes ulmi, an elongated scale that lies flat on the bark, the eggs overwinter under their dead parents old scales, usually on twigs but may move onto fruit.

San José Scale, Quadraspidiotus perniciosus, may completely coat trees, each female produces 400 young with three generations a year, even small infestations cause die back and fruit damage. Oystershell Scale, Quadraspidiotus ostreaeformis, has the obvious shaped shell, the larvae overwinter before settling down to make a scale in spring, seldom found in such numbers as the others but may then cause similar damage.

Earwigs Forficula auricularia, cause ulcerous holes in fruit messed with excreta, worst in trees surrounded by grass.

Holes with 'maggots' in the apples are probably either Apple Sawfly or Codling Moth. The sawfly, Hoplocampa testudinea, a dirty whitish caterpillar with a brown head, makes big rotten holes in the middle with a tunnel usually from the top. This is the worst pest as it may leave one and start another or even several apples and sometimes making a ribbon scar across a fruit as it travels, with each damaged fruit falling early, the larvae overwintering in the soil. The sawfly caterpillars attack from when the fruit first swells till early summer about the time of the June Drop and then through summer and early autumn it's the Codling's turn.

Suffers badly from the Codling Moth Cydia pomonella, big holes with 'maggots' in the apples in mid to late summer and a pinkish caterpillar with a brown head, these make a big mess in the middle, often enter from the side of the fruit and leaves by eye, but does at least ruin but the one fruit apiece.

Suffers the Vapourer moth Orgyia antiqua caterpillar, hairy yellow tufts on their backs, leaves egg bundles of 200 yellowish or reddish brown eggs attached with a silk cocoon. Do not touch these caterpillars as the hairs can irritate your skin.

Suffers, and avoid likewise, the Lackey moth Malacosoma neutria, a blueish grey caterpillar with red, and whitish or yellowish stripes, spin themselves a silk tent in midsummer, the eggs are laid in an obvious ring around a stem.

Suffers many Tortrix moths. Caoaecia / Archips podana, fruit-surface eating caterpillars are pale yellow and feed under a leaf they have stuck to the fruit. Cherry Bark Tortrix Enarmonia formosana is a pink caterpillar tunneling under the bark, mainly on cherries but also attacks Malus, Pyrus and Prunus trees especially those in decline. Several other closely related Tortrix moths also eat foliage, buds and damage the surface of fruits. Distinguishable by their wriggling backwards if touched these mostly hide in silk nests formed between leaf surfaces where they hide.

Suffers the Bud moth Spilonata ocellana caterpillars are small reddish brown with a black head and first ruin the buds then the foliage and finally the fruits.

Suffers the Browntail moth Euproctis chrysorrhea, caterpillars are striped red and white and hairy going grey with age, and the Small Ermine Moth Hyponomeuta (probably Yponomeuta evonymella) malinellus / malinella, small spotted caterpillars, both build silk nests in the crutches and branches and venture out to defoliate the tree.

Suffer the Fall Webworm Hyphantria cunea, light green becoming brownish with warts, caterpillars eat the underside of the leaves leaving skeletons while the droppings are caught in masses of hairy webbing they make for protection.

Suffer the Black-veined White butterfly Aporia crataegi yellow caterpillars eat the topside of the leaves and spin them together with loose webs in which they overwinter and when mature pupate attached to twigs.

Suffer the Pith moth Blastodacna atra, larvae are brownish pink with a brown head, these eat out the centres of shoots and buds which die back.

Also suffer three more moth maggots; the Winter moth Operophethora / Operophtera brumata, the March moth Erannis aescularia and the Mottled Umber Hybernia defoliaria. These are all Looper caterpillars and move by making a bend in their middle moving front and rear independently. These damage foliage and fruit from early in the season and then fall to the ground to pupate. The female Winter moth cannot fly and must crawl up the tree to lay eggs.

Suffer Apple Leaf Blister moths Lyonetia clerkella, these are very small, the adults overwinter in bark cracks and lay eggs in young leaves which are mined by green larvae, these fall with leaves in autumn to pupate and overwinter, sometimes bits of leaf drop out, and there can be up to 3 generations a year, also found on Prunus cerasus.

Suffer Apple Fruit miners Argyresthia conjugella, make wee tunnels under the skin causing sunken patches leading to rotten flesh, their alternate host is rowan / mountain ash trees.

Suffer the Leopard moth Zeuzera pyrina caterpillars, yellowish white, brown head and black spots up to two inches long bore in the wood.

Also suffer: Yellow / Gold Tail Euproctis similes / auriflua (also on fruits), Gipsy Moth Lymantria dispar, Black Arches Lymantria monacha, Pale Pinion Lithophane socia / petrificata, and Grey Dagger Apatele psi.

And also suffer the rather different Eupista species and Solenobia inconspicuella, the caterpillars of these make little cigar shaped cases in which they live and feed eating the leaves through the hole in the end making a series of overlapping little round holes making a bigger irregular patch of bare leaf.

Apples also sustain 50 less voracious and more appealing Lepidoptera larva.

One of two sustainers of 2: Pinion-spotted Pug Eupithecia insigniata / consignata (on flowers first) other being Crataegus, and Green Pug Chloroclystis rectangulata (eats flowers) other being Pyrus.

Also sustains: Scarce Swallow-tail Graphium podalirius, Eyed Hawkmoth Smerinthus ocellata, Lobster Moth Stauropus fagi, Pale Eggar Trichiura crataegii, Small Eggar Eriogaster lanestris, Chinese Character Cilix glaucata / spinula, Triple-spotted Clay Amathes ditrapezium, occasionally Brown Tail Euproctis chrysorrhoea / phaecorrhoea, Lappet Gastropacha quercifolia, Short-Cloaked Nola cucullatella, Least Black Arches Celama confusalis / cristulalis, Gothic Phalaena typical, Sprawler Brachyonycha sphinx / cassinia, Green-Brindled Crescent Allophyes oxycanthae, Dotted Chestnut Dasycampa rubiginea, Dark Dagger Apatele tridens, Lunar-Spotted Pinion Cosmia pyralina, Nut-tree Tussock Colocasia coryli, Figure of Eight Episema caeruleocephala, Blue-bordered Carpet Plemyria bicolorata / rubiginata, Red-green Carpet Chloroclysta siterata / psittacata, and Brimstone Moth Opisthograptis luteolata / crataegata. Fireblight Erwinia amylovaca is a serious bacterial infection that spreads into the wood from the initial attack usually on the flowers which look as if burnt, and eventually kills trees (though almost all susceptible varieties have already expired). Known in the USA for two centuries it arrived in the UK in 1957 and has since wiped out many of our Rosaceae. Juniper stem galls are caused by rust fungi Gymmnosporangium juniperi which moves to apple where it causes orange yellow below and red on top galls on foliage.

Powdery mildew Podosphaera leucotricha very commonly attacks young leaves and shoots leaving them narrowed, distorted, curled even withered and covered with powder and worst cases stunts buds. Similar to aphid attacks in appearance but usually earlier in the season, mildew attacks can often be disregarded unless flower buds are damaged as these then give fewer poorer fruits if any. The dead but infective shoots appear grey in winter. Some varieties, ie Cox and Bramley, are notoriously badly affected. Apple Canker Nectria galligena is a serious fungal disease, often much worse in dank stagnant overgrown conditions than in drier open sunny orchards. The spores enter through wounds, even leaf scars, causes sunken spots which rot the bark and ulcerate it exposing the wood and swelling up all round until it rings the twig, limb or even trunk and the tree dies, Cox's Orange Pippin and James Grieve are particularly troubled but Newton Wonder, Worcester Pearmain and Bramley's Seedling are much more resistant.

Scabby patches, often greenish to start with but turning dark on the fruits are usually Apple Scab Venturia inaequalis. Cox and Worcester Pearmain suffer badly whereas Charles Ross and Beauty of Bath are rarely touched. Scab is associated with canker as it often lets the latter in to do more damage on the twigs and limbs. If Scab attacks the fruits early it distorts them and cracks appear, attacking late they develop normally with only skin damage. At first the infected spots are dark, then they sink and become corky and black, sometimes perfectly round in shape. They may proliferate when apples are in store.

Very similar though not so serious is Sooty Blotch Glaeodes pomigena, dark patches looking as if the fruits have been touched with soot, often worst in damp years and shade and developing further in over-humid storage.

When the flower truss turns brown and the fruiting spur dies back it is Blossom Wilt Sclerotinia laxa, Cox and James Grieve and Lord Derby are very prone, Bramley is seldom touched.

Brown Rot Sclerotina fructigena and S. mali are fruit problems that like scab may also attack other parts. This Brown Rot is not necessarily the other brown rot of decay but rough raised rings of spots running around the fruit on the skin of a yellow cream hue that slowly mummify the fruit. Any wounds, or rough treatment causing bruising, may either get a simple rot that's brown and/or Brown Rot with the latter going on to either dry out the fruit, or, in store it may turn it black with a white fluff that allegedly infects the surrounding fruits. This is not easy to control except by ensuring minimum entrance points by careful handling, good pest control and ensuring storing fruits are picked with the pedicel (little stalk) intact. Brown Rot rarely affects Bramley's Seedling and likewise other varieties that resist canker well also resist brown rot, and the related disease Blossom Wilt. Brown Rot also affects plums similarly so keep these as far away as possible. With plums often the fruits get a brown rot with whitish bubbling but with apples it tends to stop at the flower and stem stage. Crown gall Pseudomonas tumefaciens bacteria cause cauliflower galls on the roots which hinder growth by interfering with the passage of nutrients.

An annual fungus Inonotus hispidus does much damage to old trees living on the trunk forming a large (up to 10lb) bracket of russet, whitish underneath with big pores, juicy and meaty though inedible, and dripping moisture in damp conditions, this has been used to make a yellow dye, also found on pears.

Many Viruses invade apples, often unnoticed such as Chlorotic Leaf Spot virus, Stem Pitting virus, and Scaly Bark virus. Rubbery Wood virus, a self explanatory description seen in some old specimens of a few varieties including James Grieve but particularly Lord Lambourne. Bad cases become weeping, it would be attractive in a way but the yields drop. Rubbery Wood also invades Sunset, Miller's Seedling, Worcester Pearmain, Golden Delicious.

Flat Limb is another self explanatory virus.

Mosaic virus causes a mosaic of light patterns in the leaves reducing the vigour and crop, many varieties get affected especially Bramley's Seedling, Worcester Pearmain and Lord Lambourne.

A virus is thought to cause Chats where the fruits stay small, smaller than crabs, ripen and fall early and of little use, Chat Fruit virus often invades Lord Lambourne.

Star Crack is often confused with capsid damage and it's spread by the apple capsid Plesiocoris rugicollis but is a virus infection with no control, the tiny corky patches are star shaped and as the apple expands become indented. Star Crack virus shows up most in Cox's Orange Pippin, Bramley's Seedling, Laxton's Fortune, Charles Ross, the Cox may even get the shoots killed by resultant cankers.

- ## MASLIN

An early form of companion planting; a mixed crop of wheat and rye, sometimes with peas and beans as well. Mostly used for fodder as it was difficult to separate the different crops, now returning to use as modern combine harvesters can separate the different seeds.

- ## Medicago sativa, ALFALFA / LUCERNE

A Leguminous perennial that roots deeply, accumulates Iron, Magnesium, Phosphorus (0.5%), Potassium (1.5%), Calcium (3%) as well as fixing Nitrogen.

It may yield up to eighteen tons per acre drying to about three containing nearly half a ton of mineral ash.

On a new site where alfalafa has not been grown before then this needs inoculating with companion bacteria before it will grow well, this is sold with the seed commercially. Not often a problem in gardens in Europe where the same or similar strains for beans and clover have long existed but with virgin soils it is common.

Excellent for grassed areas with deep sward, keeping it green longer in droughts as it can reach moisture inaccessible to the shallow rooted grasses. Often grown in mixture with Cocksfoot, Timothy or Meadow Fescue, but on chalky soils better mixed with Sainfoin, Wild White Clover and Italian Rye Grass. Eventually it is supplanted by dandelions as it is auto-toxic or allelopathic to itself thus it cannot be grown continuously. It performs best in a fallow, or in rotation following a corn or soya bean crop.

It is reduced in germination and growth by couch grass and yellow starthistle, and the germination inhibited by Palmer amaranth.

Root exudates from alfalfa reduce seed germination of red clover, and of Brassicas, sorghum, cucumber, cotton, wheat, lettuce and radish, and is also detrimental to their growth if they have germinated. Alfalfa residues inhibit Trichoderma virides an important soil microorganism which is now used to prevent fungal infections in woody plants.

Sustains 7 Lepidoptera larva: Pale Clouded Yellow Colias hyale, Shears Hada nana / dentina, Clouded Yellow Colias croceus / edusa, Grass Eggar Lasiocampa trifolii, Scarce Bordered Straw Heliothis armigera, Burnet Companion Eetypa glyphica, and Latticed Heath Chiasma clathrata.

Used as a sacrificial crop for corn wireworms, and for Lygus bugs on cotton but allelopathic secretions detrimental to the cotton.

Can suffer fungal Violet root rot / Copper-web Helicobasidium purpureum which also attacks asparagus, beet, carrot, parsnip, potatoes and even clover and alfalfa, and is harboured by several weeds.

Alfalafa mosaic causing necrosis and wilting also invades beans and many other plants.

Clover Yellow Vein virus; yellow mosaic, necrosis and wilting which spreads to most other Legumes and also Antirrhinum, Atriplex, Chenopodium, Coriandrum, Cucurbita, Gladiolus, Gomphrena, Nicotiana, Nicandra, Papaver, Petunia, Proboscidea, Rubus, Spinacia, Tetragonia,
and Viola.

Thrips tabaci and Frankliniella occidentalis spread Tobacco Streak virus / Bean Red Node; red nodes, necrosis and red spots, also seed borne this also spreads to chickpea, fenugreek, Datura, sweet clover, soybean, Nicotiana, most beans and many plants.

○ Melilotus arvensis, FIELD MELILOT

Leguminous. Flowers are rich in nectar.
<u>One of two sustainers</u> Small Blue Cupido minimus / alsus (eats flowers) other being Anthyllis.
Also sustains: Mazarine Blue Cyaniris semiargus / acis, Clouded Yellow Colias croceus / edusa, Grass Eggar Lasiocampa trifolii, and Mother Shipton Euclidimera mi.

May be infected by Clover Yellow Vein virus; yellow mosaic, necrosis and wilting which spreads to most other Legumes and also Antirrhinum, Atriplex, Chenopodium, Coriandrum, Cucurbita, Gladiolus, Gomphrena, Nicotiana, Nicandra, Papaver, Petunia, Proboscidea, Rubus, Spinacia, Tetragonia and Viola.

o Mentha, MINTS

These love rich moist soil, allegedly detest wood ash, and are more than somewhat invasive. Plant spearmint and table mints in pots buried in the soil to minimise their expansionist tendency.

The odour can be used to repel rodents, clothes moths, fleas and flea beetles and spearmint discourages aphids by discouraging their 'owners' the ants.

Sprays of mint tea repel ants and Colorado beetle. Mints are wonderful autumn bee plants and also aid hoverflies and predatory wasps.

One of the few plants to grow happily under walnuts these thrive near stinging nettles and benefit cabbage and tomatoes.

Mints sometimes support gorgeous metallic green shield bugs, seldom common enough to worry about. Mint Rust Puccinia menthae causes swollen shoots with yellow pustules turning brown, you can cleanse roots of the black spores for forcing or transplanting by heating them in water for 10 minutes at 112°F. Powdery mildew Oidium sp. may attack the whole plant especially in dry poor conditions.

- o **Milium effusum, SPREADING MILLET-GRASS**

Sustains Ringlet Aphantopus hyperantus.

- o **MINERAL ACCUMULATORS**

These are plants especially rich in elements. Some common plants have relatively high levels of certain elements compared to their surrounding competitors and are thus especially worth gathering for compost. This same ability also makes them tough competitors stealing away all their companions nutrients.

Boron: Euphorbias.

Cadmium: Japanese knotweed.

Calcium: Alfalfa / Lucerne, buckwheat, cabbage family, coltsfoot, comfrey, corn chamomile, corn marigold, creeping thistle, daisy, dandelion, Equisetum, fat hen, foxglove, goose-grass, great plantain, horseradish, Locust / Robinia, lupins, melons, oak bark, purslane, scarlet pimpernel, sheep's sorrel, shepherd's purse, silverweed, soya beans, stinging nettles, thistles, yarrow.

Cobalt: Bulbous buttercup, comfrey, Equisetum, ribwort plantain, rosebay willow herb, tufted vetch.

Copper: Bulbous buttercup, chickweed, coltsfoot, creeping thistle, dandelion, great plantain, ribwort plantain, sow-thistles, spear thistles, stinging nettles, tufted vetch, yarrow.

Iron: Alfalfa / Lucerne, broad beans, bulbous buttercup, chickweed, chicory, coltsfoot, comfrey, creeping thistle, dandelion, Equisetum, fat hen, foxglove, great plantain, ground ivy, groundsel, oats, silverweed, stinging nettles.

Lead: Minuartia verna.

Magnesium: Alfalfa / Lucerne, borage, coltsfoot, daisies, Equisetum, ribwort plantain, salad burnet, sheep's sorrel, silverweed, yarrow.

Manganese: Bulbous buttercup, chickweed, comfrey.

Nickel: Alyssum bertolonii.

Nitrogen: Most young growth has higher % Nitrogen than older more fibrous material, though in some such as borage may be converse. All Leguminous plants fix Nitrogen so their roots and root remains are especially useful. The following have relatively high haulm levels of Nitrogen when green: borage, broad-leaved dock, chickweed, fat hen, groundsel, knotgrass, purslane, sow-thistles, stinging nettles.

Phosphorus: Alfalfa / Lucerne, broad beans, thorn-apple, valerian, vetches, yarrow.

Potassium: Alfalfa / Lucerne, Artemesias, broad-leaved dock, bulbous buttercup, cabbages, chickweed, chicory, coltsfoot, comfrey, corn chamomile, couch grass, fat hen, goose-grass, great plantain, horse radish, purslane, stinging nettles, Tagetes, tansy, thistles, vetches, yarrow.

Selenium: Astragalus.

Silica: couch grass, dandelion, great plantain, Equisetum, knotgrass, sheep's sorrel, stinging nettles.

Sulphur: Alliums, Brassicas, coltsfoot, fat hen, horseradish, purslane.
Zinc: Japanese knotweed, Thlaspi.

- ○ **Molinia caerula, PURPLE MOOR GRASS**

<u>Sole sustainer of</u> Marbled White-Spot Jaspidia pygarga / fasciana / fuscula. <u>One of two sustainers</u> Scotch Argus Erebia aethiops / blandina / medea other being Aira caespitosa.
Also sustains: Large Heath / Marsh Ringlet Coenonympha tullia / davus / tiphon, Drinker Philudoria potatoria, Antler Cerapteryx graminis, and Crescent Celaena leucostigma / fibrosa (in stems).

- ○ **Morus nigra, MULBERRY**

Slow growing large trees with delicious fruit loved by birds.
Often one of last trees to come into leaf in spring, and stays in leaf late in autumn.
Can be pollarded, coppiced and hard pruned for fodder. M. alba is the better species for sustaining real silkworms.

○ MUSHROOMS, CULTIVATED

Usually grown on fermented horse manure the common edible mushroom Agaricus / Psalliota campestris needs constant temperatures and humidity. A cellar or cave is ideal, I found the bilges of a houseboat worked well. Cracking of the caps is simply too dry conditions.

Rose Comb is a symptomatic result of some pollution causing the cap to distort to a hen comb shape.

The mushrooms are often ruined by Sciarid and Phorid flies whose larvae tunnel through the stems and caps. Springtails / Brown fleas, Fungus Gnats and several mites also prove troublesome.

Several fungi attack the desired mushrooms; White Mould / Bubbles disease is Mycogone perniciosa which coats the mushrooms with a white mould and they become stunted and distorted. Brown Blotch is a stain on the cap from Pseudomonas tolaasii.

The mycelium in the bed is competed with by White Plaster mould Monilia / Oospora fimicola which looks as if plaster has been scattered on the surface. Brown Plaster mould Papulaspora byssina / Myriococcum praecox first makes white matted or fluffy patches and these brown and go powdery. Mushroom-bed Sclerotium fungus Xylaria vaporaria forms white threads and black sclerotia (have smell of cucumber) which can be pulled up if the protruding end (often pink) can be spotted. Mushroom-bed Brackets are the toadstool fungus Clitocybe dealbata with white stems, caps and gills.

Common soil microbes Vertcillium spp. Fusarium spp. and Cephalosporum spp. can invade the mushroom mycelium.

○ Nardus stricta, MAT-GRASS

<u>Sole sustainer of</u> Mountain Ringlet Erebia epiphron / cassiope.
<u>One of two sustainers</u> Feathered Gothic Tholera popularis other being Poa.
<u>One of three sustainers of 2:</u> Hedge Rustic Tholera cespitis others being Aira species, and Straw Underwing Thalpolphila matura / eytherea others being Aira and Poa species.
Also sustains: Small Heath Coenonympha pamphilus, and Antler Cerapteryx graminis,

○ Ocimum basilicum, BASIL

One of the tastiest herbs in the garden and a shame it needs so much warmth.
Basil dislikes rue.
It has been sprayed as an emulsion against asparagus beetle and used as a trap plant for aphids.

○ Onobrychis vicifolia, SAINFOIN / ESPARSETTE

A Leguminous plant once more widely grown now still occasionally seen as field crop or green manure.

The dried plant yields 6.25% ash containing 0.53% phosphoric acid and 1.3% lime.

Flowers said to make poor wax but delicious honey.

Aids most other plants and as a garden perennial can be included in borders and edges. It may help when sown in small proportion with cereals. Was sown mixed with small quantity of Wild White Clover (to suppress weeds especially Slender Foxtail).

It has been sprayed as an emulsion against asparagus beetle and used as a trap plant for aphids.

Sustains: Queen of Spain Fritillary Argynnis lathonia, Latticed Heath Chiasma clathrata, and Bloxworth Blue Everes argiades / tiresias (eats flowers, seeds and leaves).

- ### Origanum, MARJORAM / OREGANO

Copious flowers rich in nectar.

All this family are beneficial with strong aromatic oil that makes them favourites in the kitchen. Best flavoured Orgeanos are sadly tender.

The golden form of Marjoram only turns yellow when the sun is warm and bright enough and makes a cheerful and beneficial ground cover.

The oil gives some control over Botrytis Grey mould.

Sustains 10 Lepidoptera larva.

One of two sustainers Lace Border Scopula ornata / paludata other being Thymus.

Also sustains: White Point Leucania albipuncta, Mullein Wave Scopula marginepunctata / promutata / incanata, Lewes Wave Scopula immorata, Sub-angled Wave Scopula nigropunctata / strigilaria, Green Carpet Colostygia pectinataria / viridaria, Shaded Pug Eupithecia subumbrata / scabiosata, Wormwood Pug Eupithecia absinthiata / minutata, Black-veined Moth Siona lineata / dealbata, and Double-striped Pug Gymnoscelis pumilata (eats flowers)

cabaage and other plants especially lettuce.

o **Oryza sativa, RICE**

Strongly self inhibitory, all residues must be broken down before next crop can germinate- thus rice is usually not sown in situ but transplanted into place. Also inhibits soya beans.

Croton bonplandianum exudates seriously reduce rice germination.

Borreria articularis, an Asian weed, suppresses its growth, as does Purple nutsedge exudates and volatile allelopaths from Lantana camara, Ocimum sanctum, Tridax procumbens and Cyperus rotundus.

o **Panicum crus-galli, COCKSPUR**

This grass exudes substances suppressing germination of cabbages, carrots and tomatoes.

○ Panicum miliaceum, RED MILLET

Both germination and growth inhibited by yellow
starthistle.

○ Panicum virgatum

Establishment from seed hindered by sandbur
Cenchrus longispinus.

○ Pastinaca sativa, PARSNIP

Very slow germination, fresh seed is needed every
year.
These grow well with lettuce and peas if not shaded
too much.
The seeds have high levels of allelopathic
compounds that inhibit germination of seeds of
many plants and also contain antibiotics which
protect them against Botrytis, liquid extracts have
proved protective to French beans.
The flowers attract hoverflies and predatory wasps
and make a sacrificial crop against Carrot Blossom
moths as liked by Carrot Root fly Psila rosae , see
carrots.
Foliage attacked by Celery and Parsnip Fly Tephritis
/ Trypeta onopordinis.

The flowerhead of the wild species may be attacked by Dipteron gall-midge Kiefferia / Schizomyia / Asphondylia / Cecidomyia pimpinellae which causes the walls to thicken and the ovary to swell considerably, greenish yellow to purple or brown, but as parsnips are seldom flowered this does not often get seen in gardens.

One of three sustainers White-spotted Pug Eupithecia tripunctaria / albipunctata (eats flowers) others being Angelica and Heracleum.

Also sustains Small / Garden Swift Moth Hepialus lupulinus (roots).

Main problem for parsnips is Canker, also called Rust, usually a mixture of diseases rotting tissues after some wound or crack allows entry especially of Bacterium carotavorum.

Leaf Spots of Ramularia pastinacae, small brown spots, rarely serious unless over-crowded.

Sclerotinia Rot can be serious, see carrots, Daucus. Parsnips may get Downy mildew which damages leaves with pale spots whitish underneath, Powdery mildew is more common, caused by Erysiphe polygoni which has various strains each attacking specific plants, use fresh seed and improve hygiene.

- ○ **Pennisetum typhoides / typhoideum, PEARL MILLET / BAJRA**

Growth inhibited by Asian weeds Echinops echinatus, Dicanthium annulatum and Celosia argentea and germination by Digera alternifolia and Peganum harmala. Leaf leachate of Pluchea lanceolata an Asian weed hinders growth. Tephrosia purpurea, an Indian weed, is very inhibitory of germination and growth.

- ○ **Petroselinum hortense, PARSLEY**

Health giving herb that loves moist soil, difficult to establish or move. Let it self seed where it will.
If short of Magnesium leaves become pale, marbled with a purplish hue.
As a camouflage plant it has often been used to mask carrots and onions from their root flies though it suffers from Carrot Root fly itself, see carrots.
Sow parsley in meadows to attract hares.
Apparently toxic to parrots.
Aids tomatoes and asparagus making a happy trio but only if enough water is present, though some varieties of tomato may not get on with parsley.
It has been sprayed as tea against asparagus beetles.
Like dill, supposedly loved by bees especially prosopis ones, but I find it attracts more hoverflies.
Grown under roses it will repel their Aphis.

Parsley seeds contain antibiotics which protect them against botrytis, liquid extracts have proved protective to French beans.

Sustains Mouse Amphipyra tragopogonis.

Suffers Leaf Spot Septoria petroselini causing small brown spots going white with black dots, commonly seed borne.

Rust Puccinia aethusae occurs with rusty pustules under the leaves in summer and more, darker ones in autumn.

- ## Phaseolus coccineus, RUNNER BEANS

South American perennials and tender though their roots can be over-wintered as one can with Dahlias for an earlier though light crop.

They can shade out other crops though may benefit some, especially celery and saladings, but only when enough water is available.

Inhibited by onions these beans have the same affinities as most other beans.

Their exudates suppress germination and growth of many weeds. They dislike kohlrabi and sunflowers but will grow well with and up sweet corn which they protect from corn armyworms (US co-life).

They get on with most Brassicas, especially Brussel's sprouts, which are sheltered while small and then grow on once the beans die back flourishing on the Nitrogen left by them.

The flowers are often bitten into by buff-tailed and small earth humble bees whose tongues are too short to reach the nectar by legitimate means, this results in reduced pollination of the seeds and so flowers produce pods with fewer seeds than the standard or just abort.

Red spider mite can be a problem in hot dry years. Anthracnose and rarely Halo blight may attack as on French beans, see below.

- ## Phaseolus vulgaris, DWARF / FRENCH / HARICOT BEANS / WAX-POD / SNAP / STRING / GREEN

These beans came from South America but have spread worldwide.

Mostly dwarf there are running / climbing forms of these which give more per sq. ft.

These do well with celery when planted in rich moist soil and produce earlier crops when with strawberries which also benefit.

Rye exudates inhibit their growth as does couch grass.

Brassicas interplanted with French beans significantly reduces pest levels on both.

Prone to Red Spider mite in hot years and under cover.

The Bean Seed fly Delia cilicrura lays eggs in the soil close to the plants the whitish larvae tunnel into the stems and seeds, the adult is often attracted by decaying material, also attacks runner beans.

The Bean beetle Bruchus rufimanus, the Pea beetle B. pisorum and the Broad Bean beetle Acanthoscelides obtectus all cause holes and transparent patches in the seeds, the adults lay eggs on the pods and the larvae eat into the seeds, the pupae may not be noticed in saved seed and then sown with the next crop.

The Root knot eelworm can cause their roots to get galls the size of dots to as big as plums.

Parsley and parsnip seeds contain antibiotics that protect against Botrytis, liquid extracts have proved protective to French beans. Dutch researchers have found that French beans could also be protected from Botrytis by coating them with certain yeasts. These may occur naturally when honeydew from aphid infestations on other plants drips onto them, an interesting concept in crop protection.

At Ryton Gardens they have shown that interplanting Brassicas with French beans significantly reduces pest levels on both.

Anthracnose often miscalled canker, rust or blight, Colletotrichum lindemuthianum, causes specks, spots and lesions, dark brown sunken cankers and die back on all parts, worse in wet years and under glass, spots on pods start reddish brown and enlarge, become slimy then infect seeds, which should not be resown.

Halo Blight, Bacterium medicaginis / Pseudomonas phaseolicola is spread by rain, the semi-transparent spots on leaves surrounded by pale yellow halo, if joining together the leaves become brown and wither, even the stems may succumb and the plants wilt, also damage to seeds, this is seed carried so do not sow seeds with blisters, also attacks runner and other beans.

Root rots, Fusarium solani and others, cause plants and or crop to simply fail.

Leaf Spots Asochyta pisi, A. pinodella and Mycosphaerella pinodes cause brown spots with darker margins especially in damp weather on leaves and pods, may stunt growth, seeds become discoloured and infected and should not be resown, overwinters on debris.

Beans are infected by a huge number of viruses worldwide spread by different vectors.

Aphids spread: Alfalafa mosaic, mottling with yellow dots, spread by fourteen species and wide range of alternate hosts. Bean Common mosaic, green mosaic with stunting, also seed spread. Bean Leaf Roll; mosaic and distortion, also invades other Legumes and is a problem with peas. Bean Yellow mosaic; dark and yellow patches with bright yellow spots which also infects many other Leguminous plants and also Alpinia, Chenopodium, Gladiolus, Freesia, Babiana, Sparaxis and Tritonia. Broad Bean Wilt; yellow mosaic and distortion (also infects spinach, lettuce, pea, broad bean and other Legumes). Blackeye Cowpea mosaic; chlorosis, necrosis and wilting, also seed spread, infects most beans. Clover Yellow Vein; yellow mosaic, necrosis and wilting which infects most other Legumes and also Antirrhinum, Atriplex, Chenopodium, Coriandrum, Cucurbita, Gladiolus, Gomphrena, Nicotiana, Nicandra, Papaver, Petunia, Proboscidea, Rubus, Spinacia, Tetragonia and Viola. Cowpea Aphid-borne mosaic: mosaic, necrosis and wilting. Cucumber mosaic; green mosaic and blisters (infects 800 plant species and in 19 is seed borne as well as aphid spread). Passionfruit Woodiness; mosaic, blisters and distortion. Pea mosaic; yellow mosaic. Peanut Mottle; necrosis and wilting. Soybean mosaic; green mosaic with stunting, blistering, leaf cupping, necrosis, wilting and death. Watermelon mosaic spread by more than 20 aphid species, usual mosaic symptoms plus pods mottle and distort, also infects many Cucurbits and Legumes.

Whiteflies spread: Melon Leaf Curl virus spread also invades Cucurbits. Bemesia tabaci spreads Bean Golden mosaic; golden mosaic and stunting, also infects wild Legumes. Same whitefly spreads Bean Dwarf mosaic; yellow mosaic and stunting, found on weeds Sida spinosa and S. rhombifolia. Euphorbia mosaic; necrotic lesions and distortion, also infects lentil, soybean and other Legumes. Rhynchosia mosaic; yellowing and stunting.

Beetles spread: Bean Curly Dwarf mosaic; mosaic, stunting and rugosity, also infects other Phaseolus species, soybean, pea, chickpea, lentil, broad bean, mung bean and Leguminous weeds. Bean Mild mosaic; green mosaic. Bean Pod Mottle; mosaic and rugosity. Bean Rugose mosaic; mosaic with severe rugosity. Bean Southern mosaic; green mosaic with rugocity also infects soybeans, cowpeas, peas and other Legumes. Blackgram Mottle; mottling and distortion. Cowpea Chlorotic Mottle / Bean Yellow Stipple; yellow spots and slight stunting, also affects other Legumes.

Leafhoppers spread: Beet Curly Top; curling, yellowing and stunting, mostly a problem in arid regions where it infects a wide range of plants. Orosius argentatus spreads Tobacco Yellow Dwarf / Bean Summer Death; yellowing and wilting.

Nematodes especially of genus Xiphinema spread: Tobacco Ringspot; mosaic, necrosis with stunting, can spread to large range of woody and herbaceous plants, as can Tomato Ringspot; mosaic, necrosis and stunting.

Thrips tabaci and Frankliniella occidentalis spread Tobacco Streak virus / Bean Red Node; red nodes, necrosis and red spots, also seed borne this also affects alfalfa, chickpea, fenugreek, Datura, sweet clover, soybean, Nicotiana, other beans and many plants.

Fungi, chytrid Olpidium Brassicae, spread Tobacco Necrosis / Stipple Streak to beans; necrosis with stunting, also affects wide range of shrubby and herbaceous plants.

Unknown vectors spread Tobacco mosaic virus to beans; necrotic local lesions, yellowish green blotches, leaves crinkle, turn down and deform.

- ## Phleum pratense, TIMOTHY/ CAT'S-TAIL GRASS

The pollen extract seriously inhibits germination of other grasses and plants.

Erica australis inhibits its germination, Sasa cernua seriously reduces germination and growth.

Eaten with relish by cows, horses and sheep.

One of three sustainers Essex Skipper Thymelicus lineola others being Agropyron repens and Brachypodium pinnatum.

Also sustains: Marbled White Melanargia galathea, Meadow Brown Maniola jurtina / janira, Large Skipper Ochlodes venata / sylvanus, and Small Skipper Thymelicus sylvestris / linea / thaumus.

○ Pisum sativum, PEAS

Have a high requirement for Manganese and may get Marsh Spot if deficient shown by seeds having dark rusty patch on cotyledons, worse in over-limed and unbalanced soils, seaweed sprays alleviate this.

Root exudates from peas increase the availability of N, P, K and Ca and they are also Leguminous.

Peas suppress fat hen, grow well near roots and beans, celeriac, potatoes, Cucurbits and sweet corn. They get on with most herbs but only where they do not cast too much shade. Peas do not like onions or other Alliums though leeks are tolerated, and Jerusalem artichokes inhibit their germination. Gladioli are supposed not to like peas.

Hot water extracts from pea seedling roots suppressed yeasts and inhibited seedlings of many plants. Gloriosa lily extracts radically altered pea germination and growth.

The large green Pea aphid Acyrthosiphon / Macrosiphum pisum / pisi feeds on leaves and stems, can wither the growing tips in summer, and spreads Mosaic virus.

The Bean beetle Bruchus rufimanus / granaria, the Pea beetle B. pisorum and the Broad Bean beetle Acanthoscelides obtectus all cause holes and transparent patches in the seeds, the adults lay eggs on the pods and the larvae eat into the seeds, the pupae may not be noticed in saved seed and then sown with the next crop.

The Pea and Bean weevil Sitrona lineata and spp. eat notches from the shoots and young leaves, as they are brownish the small adults are difficult to see especially as they often eat from the underside of leaves, the adults overwinter in the soil and lay eggs on the roots of most Leguminous plants but these cause little damage.

The Pea Midge Contarina pisi has small white jumping larvae which usually eat flowers, terminal buds and also the pods.

Pea and Bean thrips Kakothrips robustus / pisirorus causes silvering of the leaves and pods, the adults are black and tiny, the larvae yellowish, in large numbers these may stunt growth. Thrips do other damage to peas; often they start attacks at ground level on the stem stunting seedlings, destroying growing points, distorting growth and turning pods brown.

Very similar symptoms are caused by Pea eelworm nematodes Heterodera schachtii and Anguillulina dipsaci.

All aerial parts galled by nematode eelworm Tylenchus devastatrix, this causes considerable distortions, weakening and stunting.

The Pea Moth Laspeyresia nigricana gives those most annoying small greenish white grubs in the peas, very early and very late crops often miss this as the moth is flying in midsummer.

Sustain: Silver Gamma / Y Moth Plusia gamma, Pale Mottled Yellow Caradrina clavipalpis / cubicularis / quadripunctata (seeds), and Scarce Bordered Straw Heliothis armigera.

Suffers Pea Moth Laspeyresia nigricana, those most annoying small greenish white grubs in the peas, very early and very late crops often miss this as the moth is flying in midsummer.

If you are growing peas for the first time on 'virgin' soil then add the commercially supplied Legume inocculant or compost containing pea residues to ensure the right fungi and bacteria are available.

Pea Wilt Fusarium oxysporum f. pisi, F. oxysporum f. redolens, and F. solani f. pisi are seen as wilting, often at flowering time with the leaves greying and yellowing, tthen the leaves roll from the edges, if the stem is slit there is an orangey red discolouration inside, this is serious and needs burning with the roots and no peas growing there for five years! Soils containing Fusarium equiseti and other strains produce highly phytotoxic substances causing scorching of foliage and reduced growth of pea stems. Roots may also rot if attacked by F. solani, Aphanomyces euteiches, and Black-Root rot, Thielaviopsis basicola, all of which are worse in poor soil conditions especially excessive wet.

Powdery mildew, Erysiphe polygoni, powdery white deposits, also attacks swedes and turnips, but in different strains to peas, most serious late in season and especially in dry summers, this has been controlled by powdered ginger and sweet flag extracts (which also stimulated vigour).

Downy Mildew, Perenopspora viciae, greyish furry growth, seldom a problem save in very wet years.

Pod and Leaf Spots, Ascochyta pisi, A. pinodella and Mycosphaerella pinodes, spread by infected seeds and on debris, worse in wet seasons, improve hygiene and do not save seed.

Grey Mould, Botrytis cinerea, common grey furry mould worse in wet seasons and over-crowded plants, improve hygiene.

Peas suffer many viruses: Pea mosaic; yellow mosaic virus, also attacks beans, sweet peas, pale green yellowing and mottling of leaves, white spots between veins and deformation, and 'breaking' of flowers, spread by aphid Acyrthosiphon pisi.

Bean Leaf Roll virus can also attack peas where it is more serious than for beans.

Broad Bean Wilt virus; yellow mosaic and distortion spreads to lettuce, spinach, broad bean and other Legumes.

Clover Yellow Vein virus; yellow mosaic, necrosis and wilting which spreads to most other Legumes and also Antirrhinum, Atriplex, Chenopodium, Coriandrum, Cucurbita, Gladiolus, Gomphrena, Nicotiana, Nicandra, Papaver, Petunia, Proboscidea, Rubus, Spinacia, Tetragonia and Viola.

And can be infected by Bean Curly Dwarf mosaic; mosaic, stunting and rugosity, also spreads to other Phaseolus species, soybean, chickpea, lentil, broad bean, mung bean and Leguminous weeds.

Bean Southern mosaic; green mosaic with rugocity also spreads to soybeans, cowpeas and other Legumes

○ Poa annua, ANNUAL MEADOW GRASS

Annoying weed that self seeds into bare patches in swards.

Constant source of nematodes that attack many crop and ornamental plants especially Stem Eelworm Tylenchus devastatrix.

Sustains 31 Lepidoptera larva.

<u>Sole sustainer of 2:</u> Devonshire Wainscot Leucania putrescens, and Light Arches Apamea lithoxylaea.

<u>One of two sustainers of 5:</u> Feathered Gothic Tholera popularis other being Nardus, Lunar Underwing Omphaloscelis lunosa other being Holcus, Beautiful Gothic Leucochlaena hispida / oditis other being Agropyron, Anomalous Stilbia anomala other being Aira caespitosa, and Ear-Moth Hydraecia oculea / nictitans other Poa species.

<u>One of three sustainers of 2:</u> Dark Arches Apamea monoglypha / polyodon others being Agropyron repens and Dactylis glomerata, and Straw Underwing Thalpolphila matura / eytherea others being Aira and Nardus.

Also sustains: Wall butterfly Pararge megera, Marbled White Melanargia galathea, Hedge Brown / Gatekeeper Maniola tithonus, Ringlet Aphantopus hyperantus (possibly also on other Poa species), Drinker Philudoria potatoria, Antler Cerapteryx graminis, Square-spot Rustic Amathes xanthographa, Deep Brown Dart Aporophyla lutulenta, Grayling Satyrus semele, Common Wainscot Leucania pallens, Feathered Brindle Aporophyla australis, Speckled Wood / Wood Argus Pararge negeria, Southern Wainscot Leucania straminea, Meadow Brown Maniola jurtina / janira, Small Heath Coenonympha pamphilus, Feathered Ear Pachetra sagittigera / leucophaea, Clay Leucania lithargyria, Double Line Mythimna turca, Dusky Brocade Apamea obscura / gemina / remissa, Silver-Barred Eustrotia olivana / argentula / bankiana, Yellow Shell Euphyia bilineata, and possibly Reddish Light Arches Apamea sublustris though this may also eat other grasses.

- ○ **Poa nemoralis, WOOD MEADOW GRASS**

The stem is attacked by Dipteron gall-midge Poamyia poae / Hormomyia causing it to split and many dozens of adventitious roots form in two neat rows, envelop and interlace to form an oval shape about a third of an inch long, light green or brown, often the stem bends at this point, larva lives and pupates inside.

Sustains 7 Lepidoptera larvae: Speckled Wood / Wood Argus Pararge negeria, Southern Wainscot Leucania straminea, Small Heath Coenonympha pamphilus, Feathered Ear Pachetra sagittigera / leucophaea, Clay Leucania lithargyria, Double Line Mythimna turca, and Confused Apammea furva.

- ○ **Poa pratensis, BLUEGRASS / SMOOTH-STALKED MEADOW-GRASS**

The decaying residues inhibit root growth of wheat. Sustains: Meadow Brown Maniola jurtina / janina, Silver-Barred Eustrotia olivana / argentula / bankiana, and Shaded Broad-Bar Ortholitha chenopodiata / limitata / mensuraria.
Sustains: Meadow Brown Maniola jurtina / janina, Silver-Barred Eustrotia olivana / argentula / bankiana, and Shaded Broad-Bar Ortholitha chenopodiata / limitata / mensuraria.

- ○ **Poa trivialis, ROUGHISH / ROUGH-STALKED MEADOW GRASS**

Cows, horses and sheep eat this readily. Sustains: Speckled Wood / Wood Argus Pararge negeria, Southern Wainscot Leucania straminea, Grayling Satyrus semele, Meadow Brown Maniola jurtina / janina, and Confused Apammea furva.

- ○ **Portulaca oleracea, PURSLANE**

Accumulates Calcium, Nitrogen, Phosphorous, Potassium and Sulphur.
Richest plant source of omega 3 oils essential for animal nutrition.
A weed in N. America, germination hindered by Palmer amaranth residues.

- ○ **Prunus, STONE FRUITS & many ornamental trees**

Large genus with many common associated co-lives, these have been entered with those species most likely to have them, but bear in mind that there is a continuous drift to and from others.
Although most Stone fruits love lime, too much may cause pale green leaves with a yellowish tinge from a shortage of available Iron.
Many have glands at base of leafstalk providing 'nectar' to ants and other 'friends'.
Beware any variety bred as a pretty double flowered form as these often have no nectar or pollen and help few insects.
All are safest pruned in summer to avoid the fungal Silver-leaf disease.

- ### Prunus amygdalus / dulcis, ALMOND

Never plant sweet almonds near peaches, nectarines or bitter almonds or the nuts may not be sweet but bittter.

See **P.** persica peach below as these two are very similar, in particular their foliage is attacked by Peach leaf curl fungus ascomycete Taphrina / Exoascus / deformans, causing flattening and elongation of leaves, these forming baggy pouches usually bright red, then falling early.

- ### Prunus armeniaca, APRICOT

These fruit on spurs more like apples so though they may crop as bushes they're easily fan trained on warm walls and thus often suffer many more co-lives including 'greenhouse' ones.

Detrimentally affected by root secretions from oats, also but less so by tomatoes and potatoes. Alliums especially garlic chives are beneficial.

Commonly find Aphids, Mussel scale, Webspinning sawflies (sic), Capsids, and especially when on walls Red Spider mites.

Apricots tend to get symptomatic Die-back that simply needs pruning out.

Shot holes start as brown spots become holes and later form scabs and spots on shoots and fruits which ooze gum.

Mosaic virus transmitted by aphids mottles the leaves yellow and they may become brittle (be sure it's not Iron deficiency, the virus symptoms will remain unaffected by seaweed sprays).

Sustains Large Ranunculus Antitype flavicincta.

Suffers: usual Winter and Tortrix moths, Small Eggar Eriogaster lanestris, Old Lady Mormo maura, and Figure of Eight Episema caeruleocephala.

- ○ **Prunus avium, GEAN / MAZZARD / WILD CHERRY**

UK native and one of the main ancestors of SWEET CHERRIES

These make big trees, the surface running roots make them no friends to lawns, paths or drives! Also dry out the soil with these surface roots, which suppresses wheat and makes potatoes prone to blight.

Cherries sometimes suffer from interveinal yellowing due to a shortage of available manganese.

A total lack of fruit may be a lack of pollination as Cherries are most tricky however almost any sweet variety can be pollinated by a Morello if in flower at the same time.

Flowers often ruined by wet weather causes them to rot and let in several diseases. The fruits also split easily when rain follows a dry spell while swelling.

A mulch 12-15cm deep of shredded cherry bark and wood (no leaves) increased growth, survival rate and cropping of other tree saplings (up by 400-600%!) and much better than other half dozen mulches trialled. From the point of view of securing the crop the only co-life worth considering is the birds.

Cherries suffer Capsids and Mussel scale (see under Malus) and the same Sawflies that bother pears and plums also attack cherries, see pears.

If our climate warms more the Cherry Fruit fly Rhagoletis cerasi may become more common in the UK though seldom seen here at current time, it lay it's white maggots in the fruits which go soft and brown around the stalk and rotten inside, the maggots drop to pupate in the ground overwinter. Terminal leaves are attacked by Homopteran aphid Cherry Black-fly Myzus cerasi, eggs overwinter in bark and aphids start on new leaves and apical buds causing distorted, reddened, folded and crumpled leaves, even halting the growth entirely, in summer these aphids move onto Galium spp. bedstraws and Veronica speedwells then return to lay eggs in autumn. Cherries may crop despite suffering these devastating attacks, and the aphid attack often 'turns into' ladybirds, which go on to patrol the rest of the garden.

Sustain 26 Lepidoptera larva.

One of two sustainers White Pinion-spotted Bapta bimaculata / taminata other being Crataegus oxycantha.

Also sustains: Large Tortoiseshell Nymphalis polychloros, Black-veined White Aporia crataegi and like most cherries suffers Scarce Swallow-tail Graphium podalirius and Grey Arches Polia nebulosa (after hibernation).

Cherry Fruit moth Argyresthia curvella / nitidella caterpillars, clear green with brown head, enter the flowerbuds and eat those and the fruitlets, fall to ground pupate and emerge within two months to lay eggs in bark crevices and bud scales, the larvae emerge in two batches, some immediately when they eat till they overwinter in silk cocoons hidden in the bark, and another set that wait to hatch later in spring.

Cherry Bark Tortrix Enarmonia formosana is a pink caterpillar tunneling under the bark, may also attack apple, pear and plum trees especially those in decline.

Likewise Apple Leaf Blister moths Lyonetia clerkella are also found on cherries, very small, the adults overwinter in bark cracks and lay eggs in young leaves which are mined by green larvae, these fall with leaves in autumn to pupate and overwinter, sometimes bits of leaf drop out, and there can be up to three generations a year.

Occassionally sustains: Alsophila aescularia, Coleophora coracipennella, Cydia funebrana, Epinotia signatana, Hedya dimidioalba, H. pruniana, Lomographa bimaculata, Pandemis cerasana, Scythropia crataegella, Swammerdamia caesiella, and Yponmeuta padella.

Suffers: Small Eggar Eriogaster lanestris, Old Lady Mormo maura, and Figure of Eight Episema caeruleocephala.

Gummosis seen as gloop oozing from cracks in the bark with yellowing leaves and dieback may be Bacterial Canker, Pseudomonas mors-prunorum & P. prunicola often made worse by water logging especially on acid or heavy land, infection occurs in autumn through wounds and kills twigs, stems even branches, the first sign may be yellowing withering leaves often upwards curling.

Cherry Leaf Spot / Cherry Blight / Shot-hole disease Blumeriella jaapi / Cylindrosporium padi / Coccomyces hiemalis is a fungal disease common in US and Europe mostly on Sour cherries, overwinters on fallen leaves, infection can cause early leaf fall even before the cherries ripen.

Shot Hole Disease (not Shot-hole disease above) Clasterosporium carpophilum casues small round holes in the leaves and sunken red rimmed spots on the fruit which then shrivels, it overwinters in lesions on stems and may cause premature leaf fall.

The fruits and flowers are attacked by Brown Rot Sclerotinia fructigena & S. laxa, may attack leaves then cause Blossom Wilt, next, on flowers and rots fruit, see Malus.

Cherries are often badly attacked by Blossom Wilt Sclerotinia laxa with flowers and leaves dying with no obvious cause even buds remaining unopened and all looking as if scorched.

Cherries suffer Gloeosporium Rot Gloeosporium fructigenum and other species where the fruits turn brown and shrivelled on the tree or in store, it is a fungal infection living on small cankers on the shoots which shower spores onto the fruits.

Rarely the leaves suffer Cherry Leaf Scorch Gnomonia erythrostoma turning yellow then brown and hang on all winter to re-infect the next crop in spring, the fruits may get small hard black spots in the flesh, wild trees often harbour this disease.

Cherry Leaf Curl Taphrina cerasi is similar fungal attack to peach leaf curl and causes discolooured leaves, early leaf fall and a Witches Broom effect in cherries with stems proliferating where a leading bud was stunted.

Silverleaf disease Stereum purpureum is not such a big problem for cherries as for plums, poor growth, die back and poor cropping are indications but the confirming sign is that silvery look to the leaves in summer when an air gap forms under the membrane, fruitng bodies later form on affected branches.

Cherries are often invaded by viruses unnoticed.

Leaf Roll virus can kill mature trees which often 'seem to have died of drought'.

Tatter Leaf virus appears in early years, it's spread on pollen, symptoms disappear but cropping may be reduced up to 50% for life.

Little Cherry virus appears in many varieties especially Waterloo, often in Kanzan.

Rasp-Leaf virus is a lethal combination of two less virulent viruses, the result of soil borne infection carried by nematode eelworms; Prune Dwarf, itself pollen spread, combined with either Raspberry Ringspot or Arabis Mosaic. Either these also appears in raspberries and strawberries and the Arabis Mosaic in blackcurrants. And Prune Dwarf also causes Sour Cherry Yellows, six weeks after flowering leaves yellow and shed, often after warm days and cool nights.

- ## Prunus cerasifera, MYROBALAN PLUM

Reliable insipid fruit, the bushes make good informal hedges with sacrificial crops to other fruits.

- ## Prunus cerasus, SOUR CHERRY

More slender and twiggy than Sweet cherries these may also be pruned more easily and less riskily, self fertile.
One of the few succulent fruits that is often not eaten by wasps if others are available.
Cherry Leaf Spot / Cherry Blight / Shot-hole disease Blumeriella jaapi / Cylindrosporium padi / Coccomyces hiemalis is a fungal disease common in US and Europe mostly on Sour cherries, overwinters on fallen leaves, infection can cause early leaf fall even before the cherries ripen.

Morello Sour cherries in particular often badly attacked by Blossom Wilt Sclerotinia laxa with flowers and leaves dying with no obvious cause, even killing unopened flower buds, all looking much like they have been scorched. This often follows wet weather.

Cherries suffer Gloeosporium Rot Gloeosporium fructigenum and other spp. where the fruits turn brown and shrivelled on the tree or in store, it is a fungal infection living on small cankers on the shoots which shower spores onto the fruits.

Silverleaf disease Stereum purpureum is seldom such a big problem for cherries as for plums; poor growth, die back and poor cropping are indications but the confirming sign is a silvery look to the leaves in summer when an air gap forms under the membrane, fruiting bodies later form on affected branches.

- ○ **Prunus domestica, PLUM / DAMSON / GAGE**

These need some lime in their soil.

In years that escape the frosts all the plum family tend to crop so heavily they break branches and or exhaust the tree so thin early with shears if necessary before the fruits swell, or prop the branches if that's too late.

Fruit Gumming is caused by stressful conditions such as hot and dry, with the fruits oozing a clear chewy gum in droplets and leaving gummy lumps when cooked.

Keep away from Anemones as share a common fungal disease.

US reports garlic protects them from their Curculio beetles.

Birds and Wasps are always troublesome to the sweeter fruits and leave us the sour and unripe.

The common, annoying, co-life is maggots in the fruits. Whitish greeny yellowish with a brown or orange head is the Plum Sawfly Hoplocampa minuta and H. flava which lay in the flowers and the larvae, creamy white with yellow brown head, eat inside the fruitlets, destroying up to five apiece, then fall and pupate in the soil underneath. Prefers Czar and Victoria, spurns Ponds Seedling and Monarch.

A similar and more common problem is the Plum Fruit moth Laspeyresia funebrana whose pinkish larvae are found inside the first ripening fruits, the larvae fall to pupate and start a second generation which overwinters in a cocoon in the ground.

Anuraphis padi aphids can curl the leaves. Mealy aphids, especially Brachycaudus helichrysi / Hyalopterus arundinis completely coat the underside of leaves which also curl, with crop reduction and withered shoots, these then move to their alternate host of China asters Callistephus which may be stunted seriously.

Brown scale Euleconium corni lay 2000 eggs each, these hatch in autumn hide in the bark, move to leaves and shoots in spring where they settle to form scales, they not only suck sap but their honeydew and sooty mould hinders lower leaves.

The Red Legged Weevil Otiorhynchus clavipes found on currants and raspberries sometimes moves onto plums where it eats flowers, fruitlets, leaves even the bark of tender stems.

Capsid bug Lygus pabulinus causes the foliage to be spotted and pitted and seldom bothers fruits much.

Leaf-blade attacked by acarine gall-mite Eriophyes / Phytoptus similis causing odd little protuberances on the leaves, when up to sixty galls, yellow, orange or purplish, mostly on upperside, oval but coalescing, this also attacks Bullaces.

Whole branches and limbs dying or with tunnelled bark and wood, often with an odd smell, may have Shot-hole Borer Anisandrus dispar beetles, tiny black beetles whose larvae bore almost any fruit tree though mostly preferring Stone fruits, and in particular plums already carrying Bacterial canker, these have two broods a year.

Cherry Bark Tortrix Enarmonia formosana is a pink caterpillar tunneling under the bark, mainly on cherries but also attacks apple, pear and plum trees especially those in decline.

Sustains 25 Lepidoptera larva: Scarce Swallow-tail Graphium podalirius, Black-veined White Aporia crataegi, Lappet Gastropacha quercifolia, Large Ranunculus Antitype flavicincta, Short-Cloaked Nola cucullatella, Twin-Spotted Quaker Orthosia munda, Dark Dagger Apatele tridens, Sycamore Apatele aceris, Red Underwing Catocala nupta, Blue-bordered Carpet Plemyria bicolorata / rubiginata, Copper Underwing Amphipyra pyramidea, and occasionally Brown Tail Euproctis chrysorrhoea / phaecorrhoea.

Commonest Lepidoptera co-life is usually the Plum Fruit moth Laspeyresia funebrana whose pinkish larvae are usually found inside very early ripening fruits, the larvae fall to pupate and start a second generation which after ruining more fruit overwinter in cocoons in the ground.

Suffers: most of the caterpillars that bother apples as these also attack plums: Leopard moths, Lackey moths, Winter moths, Tortrix moths, occasionally an errant Codling Moth, Gipsy Moth Lymantria dispar, Cream-spot Tiger Arctia villica, Pale Pinion Lithophane socia / petrificata, Grey Dagger Apatele psi, Small Eggar Eriogaster lanestris, Old Lady Mormo maura, and Figure of Eight Episema caeruleocephala.

Bacterial Canker causes stunted shoots yellowing and withering leaves with shot hole like spots and cankers ulcerating limbs, the ubiquitous Victoria is often badly attacked, as is Csar. This fungus also attacks the leaves causing Shot-hole and Leaf Spot especially in wet years.

If there is die back with small but no large canker to be seen and with tiny hairs or jelly like pimples it may be Branch Die-back Diaporthe perniciosa / Dermatea prunastri.

Brown Rot / Blossom Wilt Sclerotinia / Monilia Laxa and Monilia fructigena cause the same interrelated nest of symptoms as on apples with Withered Tips, Twig Blight and cankers, and rotten, dropped and mummified fruits. Brown Rot Sclerotina fructigena, S. laxa, and S. mali can attack most parts like scab. It is known as Blossom Wilt when the flower truss turns brown and the fruiting spur dies back. This Brown Rot is not necessarily the other brown rot of decay but the fruits get a brown rot with whitish bubbling.

Sooty Blotch Glaeodes pomigena similar to that in apples causes round brown patches on the fruit skins and worst in wet years.

Silverleaf disease Stereum purpureum is a big problem for plums, you seldom see an old plum tree; poor growth, die back and poor cropping are indications but the confirming sign is a silvery look to the leaves in summer when an air gap forms under the membrane, fruitng bodies later form on affected branches. Trichoderma virides, a fungus parasitic on others can be injected into the trees to prevent such attacks but is not available to amateurs in the UK. An important point is to avoid pruning any of these or other Stone fruits, or their ornamental forms, any time other than in summer in dry conditions to prevent the fungus gaining access via the wounds. Any winter damage should be pruned back immediately and I cauterise the wounds with a blowtorch before sealing with a suitable compound, such as beeswax melted and applied with a brush. Plum fruits are attacked by Plum Leaf Curl fungus ascomycete Taphrina pruni / Ascomyces / Exoascus / institiae, causing it to shrivel and go brown, the leaves are curled and blistered, the fungus overwinters on the bark. This is also believed to cause Bladder bullace / Pocket plum / Starved plum / Mock plum, causing flattening and elongation of fruit, kernel fails and flesh inedible, pale green, greyish or dusty orange and up to two and a half inches in size. Similar fungal attacks may be found on most others in prunus family.

As with most plants mottled leaves indicate a Mosaic virus spread by aphids with no cure.

Plum Pox is another similar virus causing mottling and blueish or reddish depressed rings and spots on the fruits which then also lack sugar.

Prune Dwarf appears in Italian Prune, Switzen, causing leaf distortion and stunting but in most cultivars shows as poor leaf colour with cropping 70-80% reduced.

Bark Split virus, self descriptive, often invades Cambridge Gage more than others.

o Prunus institia, BULLACE

Sustains: Dotted Chestnut Dasycampa rubiginea, Dark Chestnut Conistra ligula / spadicea, and Lunar-Spotted Pinion Cosmia pyralina.

Suffers: Small Eggar Eriogaster lanestris, Old Lady Mormo maura, and Figure of Eight Episema caeruleocephala.

o Prunus persica, PEACH / NECTARINE

Peaches benefit from Alliums growing underneath, rich mulches, Equisetum tea and seaweed sprays. Although these love lime too much causes Chlorosis with pale green leaves with a yellowish tinge due to lack of available Iron.

Usually self fertile, surprisingly easy to grow from seed, may fruit in four or five years and often come nearly 'true'.

Do well in big tubs housed outdoors till late winter, brought under cover for flowering and fruiting, then going out again for autumn and into winter. This handicaps most of their co-lives and reduces the pruning. Permanent housing under cover is strongly not recommended as they will not get a winter chill and fail to thrive, to say little of their co-lives proliferating!

Remember these are fruits that over-cropping spoils. If you want sweet luscious globes then thin early, thin often and never leave two fruitlets closer than a hand width apart. Be especially vigilant at splitting doubles as these never swell cleanly.

Often total losses of bloom from frost, and the fruitlets remain sensitive weeks after setting.

Although these need lime too much may cause Chlorosis with pale green leaves with a yellowish tinge due to a lack of available Iron.

A shortage of lime can cause soft or Split Stones, which as name suggests split and open the flesh at the flower end helping infestation by moulds and earwigs.

In dry years it's wasps, and in wet years rot's spoil the crop, surprisingly birds are seldom a problem. With Nectarines it's the weather, even here in East Anglia these seldom ripen outdoors without at least a warm wall. Except for exceptional summers better move these under cover from late winter till just after harvest.

Ants can be their usual annoying selves and will farm scale.

Aphids cause the leaves to curl, and several different species abound.

Leaves often have the somewhat polyphagous Peach Potato Aphis Myzus persicae, amber, yellow, red even black, which alternates with many plants especially thistles. The Mealy Peach aphid Hyalopterus amygdali, amealy greeny amber, migrates to live on reeds.

The Peach aphid Appelia / AnurAphis schwartzi, greenish yellow to brownish pink, and the Black Peach aphid Brachycaudus persicaecola are less common and unusually these remain on the peaches overwinter.

Webspinning sawfly Neurotoma nemoralis larvae, green with black heads, make tents to feed on the leaves inside.

Capsids may do some damage, and on walls of course expect Red Spider mites and Mussel Scale (see under Malus).

Earwigs are a secondary problem, if the flower end of the stone splits they get in and eat out the kernel while the flesh remains fine. Take note- if you don't spot the small split in the flower end then you can enjoy the bizarre experience of biting into the sweet flesh to suddenly find your mouth wriggling with earwigs; macabre!

Suffer: usual Winter and Tortrix moth culprits and Knotgrass Apatele rumicis, Small Eggar Eriogaster lanestris, Old Lady Mormo maura, and Figure of Eight Episema caeruleocephala.

Shot Holes Clasterosporium carpophilium start as brown spots become holes and later also forming scabs and spots which appear on shoots and fruits and which may ooze gum.

Peach Powdery mildew Spaerotheca pannosa var. persicae may cause greyish white powdery patches on the leaves and shoots and reduces yields, it overwinters on buds and may severely stunt growth.

Peaches are very prone to Peach Leaf Curl, the foliage is attacked by fungus ascomycete Taphrina / Exoascus / deformans, causing flattening and elongation of leaves, forming baggy pouches usually bright red and falling early. This gets in as the buds open and swell so worst in wetter areas and thus can be prevented almost entirely by keeping the shoots dry. Permanent housing under cover eliminates this problem, then raising far too many others. Small bushes and wall trained forms can be protected overhead with a plastic sheet from mid-winter till the buds have opened. Once trees reach full size many shrug off attacks of curl anyway. This fungus visits others in family especially almond.

Mosaic virus mottles the leaves yellow, to be sure it's not chlorosis this will remain unaffected by seaweed sprays.

o **Pyrus communis, PEAR**

Mulches are especially useful and stop grass competition which is very harmful to pears. However large orchard trees may be grassed under.

A good pear is harder to grow than a good peach, these need warmth, shelter and continuous moisture. Harsh winds can blacken foliage as if burnt.

Lots of small fruits dropping may be just June Drop natural self-thinning as with apples.

Pear rust, see below, is carried over on Juniper making these bad companions.

Pears have noticeably less frequent visits of many of the same co-lives of apples; Leopard moth, Vapourer, Tortrix even Codling moths and Twig Cutters all may be found but not often, even aphids seldom bother pears.

However pears have some co-lives more their own. The Sinuate Pear Tree borer Agrilus sinuatus beetle larvae, ivory white and legless, eats mostly sapwood causing premature leaf fall and may kill branches, the larvae eat for two years then pupate in situ before the adult leaves to mate and lay eggs.

White tents formed in the leaves in summer with many caterpillars, orangey yellow with pale brown stripes and black heads, that exude a red fluid if disturbed are the Social Pear Sawfly Neurotoma flaviveniris, these also visit plums and cherries.

If the leaves are looking patchy, blotchy or skeletonised then look for slug like yellow green or blackish Slug Worms / Pear Slug sawfly Caliroa cerasi larvae on the tops of the leaves.

Another sawfly Hoplocampa testudinea, a dirty whitish caterpillar with a brown head, makes big rotten holes in the middle of the fruit with a tunnel usually from the top.

Capsid bug Lygus pabulinus makes brownish black spots on the leaves and the fruits develop lumps of corky pitted tissue. Some apparently capsid damage is actually Stony Pit or Dimpled Pear, see below. May get Nut scale which is similar to Peach scale except the base of each is widened just above junction with stem, this spreads to elms, hazels, hawthorns and pyracantha.

Leaf-blade gets Pear Leaf Blister / moth (sic) attacks caused by acarine gall-mite Eriophyes pyri / piri / Phytoptus arianus / arionae / Typhlodromus pyri / small swellings on mostly upper side of leaf, yellowish green to red and purple, turn brown black and crack at maturity, may also cause irregular reddish brown pustules on fruit. This conflated with Pear Leaf Blister moths Cemiostoma scitella are very small, the adults overwinter in bark cracks and lay eggs in young leaves which are mined by the green larvae, these fall with leaves in autumn to pupate and overwinter.

Pear Leaf midge Dasyneura pyri causes the leaves to fold upwards at the edges as the eggs are laid in the folds of young leaves, several generations a year can lead to a build up with some reduction in plant growth.

Fruit may be destroyed by Dipteron gall-midge Lestodiplosis pyri / Cecidomyia / nigra / pyricol causing Black pear which seems conflated and same as Pear Gall Midge Contarinia pyrivora, eggs are laid in flowers then yellowish white larvae eat inside of fruitlets, when these blacken and fall to the ground the midges leave (to over-winter in soil), and can cause serious fruit loss.

Bryobia mite Bryobia cristatus suck sap breed rapidly and they and their damage much resemble red spider mites except they're not hairy and have longer front legs, they're on the tree in late spring and early summer and alternate living on grasses and other herbaceous plants the rest of the year.

Summer Fruit Tortrix moths Cacoecia reticulana overwintering larvae eat leaves then pupate to emerge and lay eggs in eary summer, the hatching larvae web a leaf together, usually to a fruit, and feed inside on leaf and fruit, these mature pupate and lay so that the next generation hatch in early autumn to feed before overwintering.

Sustain another 17 Lepidoptera larva.

<u>One of two sustainers</u> Green Pug Chloroclystis rectangulata (eats flowers) other being Malus.

Also sustain: Large Tortoiseshell Nymphalis polychloros, Scarce Swallow-tail Graphium podalirius, Lappet Gastropacha quercifolia, Chinese Character Cilix glaucata / spinula, Short-Cloaked Nola cucullatella, Gothic Phalaena typica, Pale-shouldered Brocade Hadena thalassina, Clouded Drab Orthosia incerta / instabilis, Dark Dagger Apatele tridens, occasionally Brown Tail Euproctis chrysorrhoea / phaecorrhoea.

Suffer Summer Fruit Tortrix moths Cacoecia reticulana whose overwintering larvae eat leaves then pupate to emerge and lay eggs in early summer, the hatching larvae web a leaf together, usually to a fruit, and feed inside on leaf and fruit, these mature pupate and lay so that the next generation hatch in early autumn to feed before overwintering.

Cherry Bark Tortrix Enarmonia formosana is a pink caterpillar tunneling under the bark, usually on cherries this also attacks apple, pear and plum trees especially those in decline.

Also suffer: Yellow / Gold Tail Euproctis similes / auriflua, Gipsy Moth Lymantria dispar, and Grey Dagger Apatele psi.

Pear suffer a rust which at another stage is also Juniper Stem Gall rust, the fungi Gymmnosporangium sabinae moves to pears where it causes the thickened pear-leaf cluster-cups on the foliage and sometimes on stems and fruits, causing serious leaf loss and poor wood ripening.

A simple weather problem is blackening and browning of the leaves from cold dry winds with or without frost, but if flowers, shoots and leaves wither back going dark brown it might be Fireblight Erwinia amylovaca. This seriously infectious bacteria was known in the USA for two centuries then arrived in the UK in 1957 and has since decimated our Rosaceae so almost all susceptible varieties such as Laxton's Superb have already long expired.

Pear Scab Venturia pirina is a fungal attack, small spots cause early leaf fall and corky spots on fruit, has similar appearance to apple scab though a different species. It may cause whole twigs to wither, if bad this lets in Pear Canker as well. Pear Canker much resembles Apple canker as the same fungus Nectria galligena attacks both. The pear suffers ulceration and swollen distorted growth in the same way, and as with apples, some varieties are more prone such as William's, Conference and Doyenne du Comice.

An annual fungus Inonotus hispidus does much damage to old trees living on the trunk forming a large (up to 10lb) bracket of russet, whitish underneath with big pores, juicy and meaty looking though inedible, and dripping moisture in damp conditions, this has been used to make a yellow dye, also spreads to apples.

Stony Pit or Dimpled Pears is a virus the fruits are smaller with dimples or pits, hard and gritty at the bottom where they are usually darker green. If only the odd fruit affected then it may well be Capsid or even weather damage. Stony Pit rarely appears in Williams' but does so severely in Beurre Hardy, Beurre d'Amanlis and Doyenne du Comice.
Pears also get invaded by Vein Yellows virus.
Blister Canker virus often invades Williams', Doyenne du Comice, and Laxton's Superb.

o **Raphanus sativus, RADISH**

Not only grown for the roots, the small seed pods are more delicious.
This crop needs to be grown rapidly to be palatable!
Analysis of dry matter; total crude ash 5.22%, N 1.85, P 0.78, K 1.3, Ca 1.81, Na 0.71.
As these are related to the cabbage family these should usually be kept apart.
Radishes detest hyssop but get on with most other plants except Pimpinella species grapes & spinach. Chervil, lettuce and peas will all get on well together with radishes. Radish benefit from nasturtium and mustard nearby.

Tomato root exudates suppress radish and their germination is inhibited by Jerusalem artichokes. Purple nutsedge inhibits growth. Eichhornia crassipes, water hyacinth, often used as mulch in hotter climes, seriously reduces germination and inhibits growth, as does leaf leachate of Pluchea lanceolata an Asian weed. Residues of barley inhibit growth.

Most important co-life is the Flea Beetle / Fly / Turnip Flea beetle, Phyllotreta / Haltica atra / nemorum / undulate, small, black or yellow striped, make so many holes in the leaves that this may kill small plants and seedlings. Deterred by damper conditions and presence of tomatoes, the adults are the problem, the larvae live in the soil on plant roots doing little harm.

Cabbage root fly can also bother radish. Erioischia Brassicae / Delia / Anthomyia radicum, eats the roots of all Brassicas, the females consume nectar of Cow parsley Anthriscus sylvestris so are most prevalent when this is flowering, most Brassica plants turn reddish purple once attacked. It is particularly damaging to radish as it tunnels in the swollen edible part. These flies can be lured to traps containing Swede root juice as bait. Interplanting lettuce, clover or Tagetes marigolds reduces infestations. Carefully fitted collars of felt or similar at ground level stop the fly climbing down the stem to the soil and prevent her laying eggs. Heavy attacks of aphids deter this fly and apparently the Garden Pebble moth caterpillar Evergestis forficalis exudes a deterrent chemical in its frass. Rove and Ground beetles also control this by eating the eggs

The roots and more often those of Wild radish R. raphaniastrum, are galled by Coleopteran weevil Ceuthorrhynchus pleurostigma / assimilis / sulcicollis a.k.a. 'Turnip and cabbage gall weevil' which forms marble sized swellings on the roots, this may seriously harm growth in young small plants and older ones may also suffer as the larval exit holes allow in other infections. This can be widespread in an area as it also spreads to Arabis, turnips, cabbages, swedes, and charlock.

Shoot apex galled by Dipteron gall-midge Dasyneura sisymbrii / Cecidomyia barbarea, this arrests normal growth causing glossy swellings and lumps, often cream, pink or reddish, worst in floral parts, serious infestations can form what look much like small raspberries, often spreads to other cruciferae such as hedge mustard, creeping yellow cress, yellow rocket, cabbage and charlock.

Suffers: Large White Pieris Brassicae, and Small White P. rapae.

Radish scab Streptomyces scabies makes scabby patches on the skin but seldom does serious harm, attacks may be reduced by mixing grass clippings or other rich organic material into the soil when sowing.

○ **Rheum rhaponticum, RHUBARB**

An ancient aphicide recipe was boiled rhubarb leaves which contain the poison oxalic acid.

The same spray was used against blackspot on roses and Red spider mites on aquilegias.

Mice show much distaste to extract of rhubarb root.

Reputed to control clubroot and root flies in Brassicas if piece of stem of rhubarb included in the sowing or planting hole, sadly tests showed only little benefit.

Sustains Knotgrass moth Apatele rumicis.

Crown Rot Bacterium rhaponticum although rare is serious, the leaves go pale, the stem bases swell and distort then all goes soft and rotten and needs destroying.

Rhubarb can be attacked by Honey fungus Armillaria mellea with the black bootstraps in the soil, a whitish mycelium and honey coloured toadstools. Grey Mould Botrytis cinerea as found in the greenhouse attacks rhubarb when it's forced in damp dirty conditions.

Brown spots, patchy and irregular are the fungal Leaf Spot Ramularia rhei.

○ Ribes, CURRANTS

Woodland plants, these need mulching and a moist root run.

They often carry aphids which cause leaf curling, usually Aphis schneideri.

They can be damaged by the Clay-colured weevil Otiorhynchus singularis, this is a night feeder like the Red-legged weevil, black with red legs. Both weevils also attack raspberries and are often found on plums. The Clay-coloured is more destructive of the two as it strips bark as well as leaves, it overwinters as the larvae and adult in the ground where the larvae eat roots.

Most Ribes suffer Currant Clearwing Sesia tipuliformis the white with a brown head caterpillar bores in the stems which wilt and the fruit fails.

Sustain another 15 Lepidoptera larva on most of the following species.

One of three sustainers of 4: Spinach Lygris mellinata / associata also on R. grossularia and R. nigrum, Phoenix Lygris prunata others being other Ribes species, Currant Pug Eupithecia assimilata others being other Ribes and Humulus, and Waved Umber Hemerophila abruptaria others being Ligustrum and Syringa.

Also sustains: Large Ranunculus Antitype flavicincta, Grey Chi moth Antitype chi, Copper Underwing Amphipyra pyramidea, Mamestra Brassicae Cabbage Moth, Common Emerald Hemithea aestivaria / strigata / thymiaria (after hibernation), Garden Carpet moth Xanthorhoe fluctuata, Comma Polygonia c-album, Mottled Pug Eupithecia exiguata, V-moth Itama wauaria, and the Magpie Abraxas grossulariata which was once more common.

- ## **Ribes grossularia, GOOSEBERRY**

Notoriously needy for Potassium often showing this with a blueish green hue and a yellowish brownish margin to the leaf

These also need Magnesium or the leaves can become pale, marbled with a purplish hue.

Occasionally a gooseberry will bear yellow flowers on thornless stems, this is the Buffalo berry rootstock.

Tomatoes may aid them.

They do not like stagnant air.

Giant berry competitors underplanted with chickweed to create cool damp conditions at the roots. I underplant with Limnanthes douglassii for those raised up on a leg with space underneath. Bullfinches love to strip the buds.

Fruits often sucked dry by wasps with the skin left hanging.

Broad beans may help keep away their sawfly which is their most significant co-life; the Gooseberry Sawfly or apparently sawflies; Pteronidea ribesii, Nematus spp. & Pristiphora pallipes, all of which first appear in late spring early summer. If you keep watch daily one leaf will suddenly have a dozen or two pinhead sized holes; each one being eaten by a wee greeny caterpillar (green spotted with black dots / pale green and black head / dark green and pale head). Having eaten the first leaf they disperse and each munches down its own shoot, rapidly, till all is totally defoliated. Within a month or so they drop to the ground, pupate, and return for up to four generations per year. Oddly the infestation frequently appears in the third or fourth year after planting then often becomes insignificant after the sixth or seventh.

If leaves turn pale yellow and look scorched and drop off check for Gooseberry Red Spider mites Bryobia ribis / praetiosa and B. rubrioculus causing a webbing on the undersurface, these may move onto other trees and shrubs.

Aphids Aphis grossulariae are dark green and feed on the tips crumpling leaves and deforming shoots.

Aphid Eriosoma ulmi lives on the roots where it has a blanket of white woolly webbing to protect it and does serious damage even killing plants.

Big bud mite Cecidophyopsis ribis of blackcurrants does not harm gooseberries much, some buds die and turn brown, but gooseberries do not appear infected by the Reversion virus.

Likewise the Leaf spot can do light damage.

However Capsids can do more crop damage than on the smaller currants through their causing corkiness and splitting the skins of the fewer gooseberry fruits.

Sickly or weak plants may well be suffering from root aphids.

Suffers the Magpie moth Abraxas grossulariata larvae overwinter in many places especially bark crevices and eat the foliage from early spring, this used to be widespread but seldom seen now.

One of three sustainers Phoenix Lygris prunata others being other Ribes species.

Also sustains: Comma Polygonia c-album, V-moth Itama wauaria, and suffers: Yellow / Gold Tail Euproctis similes / auriflua, Garden Carpet moth Xanthorhoe fluctuata.

Gooseberry Leaf Spot Pseudopeziza ribis starts as dark spots on leaves which yellow and drop, the fruit stalks and fruit may also be attacked, bad cases debilitate the bushes.

Another most significant co-life is American Gooseberry mildew Spaerotheca mors-uvae. This appears on the tips, coats the underside of the leaves with a white felting, especially when roots are dry, spreads onto berries which then crack, and also spreads to other Ribes.

European Gooseberry mildew Microsphaera grossulariae is similar but less white, usually only appears on the upper surfaces of the leaves and does not often harm fruits, the spores overwinter on fallen leaves.

Sedges and gooseberries are alternate hosts to the Gooseberry Cluster Cups fungus Puccinia pringsheimiana which cause red and orangey blisters on the leaves and fruits first resembling leaf spots, the fungus spends autumn till summer on the sedges then moves back to the gooseberry and other Ribes. Gooseberries do not seem to suffer many virus invasions except Vein Banding virus to which the variety Leveller is particularly sensitive.

○ Ribes nigrum, BLACKCURRANTS

These like wet rich conditions, and will even grow in waterlogged soil. Bullfinches love to strip their buds. Undersow with Limmnanthes douglassii to bring in many predatory co-lives. Blackcurrants are benefitted by stinging nettles nearby.

Significant co-life is an invisible pest causing 'Big bud' making big buds many times size of normal ones, these never open, and are galled by miniscule wind blown acarine gall-mite Cecidophyopsis / Eriophyes / Phytoptus ribis, this destroys fruiting even if not carrying Reversion virus as well, see below. (Variety Foxendown proved resistant to gall mites and so avoided Reversion disease and oddly Golubka and Ben Gairn were not resistant to the mites but were somehow resistant to Reversion.)
Currants commonly carry aphids which cause leaf curling usually Aphis schneideri.
The Currant-sowthistle aphid Hypermyzus lactucae causes leaves to curl downwards and stunted growth, these then migrate to their alternate host of sowthistle.
Sudden death or a slow lingering one not otherwise explainable may be Root aphids.
If the tips and leaves wither later in spring then it may be Shoot-borer beetle Lampronia capitella grubs, red turning greenish, which also move into the fruits ruining them, the cocoons are normally hidden in cracks in the bark in winter.
Leaf midges Dasyneura tetensi cause leaves to distort twist and fold similar to aphid attacks but inside are whitish orange grubs, these mature in a month or so and with four generations a year can multiply, they overwinter as pupae in the soil.
Blackcurrants also sometimes get attacked by the Gooseberry sawfly, see above.

All the currants and gooseberries occasionally suffer from Capsid bugs Lygus pabulinus similar to those attacking apples, the leaves are attacked when young and the holes expand with the leaf making them look tatterred, overwinter as eggs on the twigs.

Buds may be destroyed by Leaf and Bud eelworm nematode Aphelencoides / Aphelenchus fragariae and A. ritzemi-bosi, these cause considerable distortions, weakening and stunting and also attack strawberries. Blackcurrants may host Mussel scale, and Red spider mite in hot dry conditions, and Weevil and Looper caterpillars.

One of two sustainers Spinach Lygris mellinata / associata other being Ribes grossularia.

One of three sustainers of 2: Phoenix Lygris prunata others being other Ribes species, and Currant Pug Eupithecia assimilata others being other Ribes and Humulus.

Also sustains: Comma Polygonia c-album, Magpie Abraxas grossulariata, and V-moth Itama wauaria. Blackcurrants may host Looper caterpillars. Occasionally a Currant Clearwing moth / European Currant Borer Sesia tipuliformis caterpillar, whitish with brown head, may hollow out then live and pupate in the stems and branches often killing them. The adult is unusual in having no scales thus clear wings and so resembles a bee. This may be conflated with another or the same grub, the Blackcurrant Crown Borer Bembecia marginata, eggs are laid in summer, the larva overwinters at the base enters a cane, lives inside restricting growth and causing die back, after many months or years pupates then emerges as the Clearwing moth.

Old overgrown bushes are often infested with lots of tiny whitish pink pustulesn to the extent they resemble coral thus Coral Spot Nectria cinnabarina which is sort of decorative in an Addams family way, usally starting on stubs of deadwood or dead shoots this can spread to ruin the whole plant.

Currants suffer Currant Leaf spot Pseudopeziza / Glaesporium ribis where sticky brown patches, shiny when wet, cause browning and the leaf falls in midsummer with in bad cases a shrivelling of the current currant crop, the spores overwinter on fallen leaves.

American Gooseberry mildew Spaerotheca mors-uvae also attacks all the currants and appears on the tips, coats the underside of the leaves with a white felting, especially when roots are dry, spreads onto berries which then crack.

European Gooseberry mildew Microsphaera grossulariae is similar, also attacks currants, it is less white than the American, usually only appears on the upper surfaces of the leaves and does not often harm fruits, the spores overwinter on fallen leaves.

Sedges and blackcurrants are alternate hosts for the fungal Gooseberry Cluster Cups little spotty rusts on leaves and fruits, see gooseberries.

Currants must not be grown in some of the US states as they are an alternate host to Blackcurrant rust Cronartium ribicola, which is a.k.a. White Pine Blister rust, which seriously damages Weymouth pines and others with five needles. The rust makes yellow cushions on the underside of the leaves which brown and wither with a woolly hairyness forming and often fall early.

Running Off is when the topmost fruits fall off early, this may be viral, lack of pollination or simply light frost damage.

Blackcurrants suffer many other viruses; Yellows, Variegation, the common Gooseberry Vein Banding and worryingly some strains of Cucumber Mosaic.

The serious problem of Reversion virus infection is normally brought by the Big Bud mite, the leaves become less ornate, more stinging nettle shaped with fewer veins, darker green, and yields drop to never recover, this can be spread on pruning tools.

o Rosmarinus officinalis, ROSEMARY

The dry needle strewn conditions underneath rosemary deters seeds germinating. Generally useful as it's scent confuses many pests.
Rosemary beetles are a newish pest, they are seldom noticed but the bushes develop dead patches which are found full of dead leaves and frass.

o Rubus, BRAMBLES AND BERRIES

All have very similar co-lives especially as so many are hybrids, most are kept relatively clean by ruthless and heavy pruning.
May become infected by Clover Yellow Vein virus; yellow mosaic, necrosis and wilting which spreads most to Legumes: Cajanus, Canavalia, Cassia, Cicer, Crotolaria, Dolichos, Glycine, Hedysarum, Lathyrus, Lens, Lupinus, Medicago, Melilotus, Phaseolus, Trifolium, Trigonella, Vicia, and Vigna, and also to Antirrhinum, Atriplex, Chenopodium, Coriandrum, Cucurbita, Gladiolus, Gomphrena, Nicotiana, Nicandra, Papaver, Petunia, Proboscidea, Spinacia, Tetragonia and Viola.

- o **Rubus fruticosus, and others, BLACKBERRIES, LOGANBERRIES et al**

Remarkably vigorous these remain productive for longer than most other soft fruits, true blackberries more than their more raspberry like hybrids.

The former true ones may sometimes crop on side-shoots off old wood, hybrids rarely do. Thornless varieties seldom crop as well as thorny forms.

Seeds become inedible as they mature, microscope reveals they are covered with tiny fish-hooks which become more indigestible as they ripen!

These may aid grapevines and certainly provide a sacrificial crop at the same time as the grapes ripen. May be aided by tansy and stinging nettles. After clearing brambles the soil will be in good heart and especially suitable for trees but regrowth will be a problem.

Their bushes are sanctuaries in nature, small birds and creatures can hide inside protected by the arching thorns, the centres are often bone dry and provide a good place to nest or hibernate.

The late flowering bramble caters for insects in early autumn when food is getting short and the fruit then feeds birds till winter.

Corky and dried up parts to fruits with little white maggots are attacks of Raspberry beetle Byturus tomentosus which commonly does more harm to the fruits of loganberries and similar hybrids than to raspberries.

Capsids Lygus pabulinus suck the foliage which is often badly damaged with large holes formed.

Aphids may do damage similar to that on currants.

Sustain 44 Lepidoptera larva.

Sole sustainer of Peach Blossom Thyatira batis.

One of three sustainers Scarce Footman Eilema complana(algae and leaves) others being Abies and Prunus spinosa.

Also sustains: Grizzled Skipper Pyrgus malvae / alveolus, Buff Arches Habrosyne pyritoides / derasa, Scarce Vapourer Orgyia recens / gonostigma, Brown Tail Euproctis chrysorrhoea / phaecorrhoea, Oak Eggar Lasiocampa quercus, Grass Eggar Lasiocampa trifolii, Fox Moth Macrothylacia / Bombyx rubi, Emperor Saturnia pavonia / carpini, Dotted Clay Amathes baia, Six-striped Rustic Amathes sexstrigata / umbrosa, Green Arches Anaplectoides prasina / herbida, Powdered Quaker Orthosia gracilis, Brown-Spot Pinion Anchocelis litura, Light Knotgrass Apatele menyanthidis, Scarce Dagger Apatele auricoma, Saxon Hyppa rectilinear, Small Grass Emerald Chlorissa viridata, Beautiful Carpet Mesoleuca albicillata, Hedge Dagger Acronycta psi, Common Pug Eupithecia vulgata, occasionally Blossom Underwing Orthosia miniosa, and Portland Ribbon Wave Sterrha degeneraria, possibly Dotted-Border Wave Sterrha sylvestraria / straminata, V Pug Chloroclystis coronata (eats flowers), Rosy Marbled Hapalotis venustula (eats flowers), Holly / Azure Blue Celastrina argiolus (in autumn)(eats flowers, flower buds, green berries and leaves), and Green Hairstreak Callophrys rubi (eats flowers and leaves).

In spring, after hibernation, brambles sustain some Lepidoptera larva that were sustained by other plants the previous autumn: Purple Clay Diarsia brunnea, Ingrailed Clay Diarsia festiva / primulae, Triple-spotted Clay Amathes ditrapezium, Silvery Arches Polia hepatica / tincta, Double Square-spot Amathes triangulum, Great Brocade Eurois occulta, Grey Arches Polia nebulosa, Early Thorn Selenia bilunaria / illunaria, Little Thorn Cepphis advenaria. Suffers: Jersey Tiger Euplagia quadripunctaria / hera, Scarlet Tiger Panaxia dominula, Pale Pinion Lithophane socia / petrificata, and Beautiful Arches Eumichtus satura. Yellow / Gold Tail Euproctis similes / auriflua, on it's fruits, and a Tortrix caterpillar, Bramble Shoot Webber Notocelia uddmanniana, first whitish then brownish red with a black head, webs the leaves together and destroys the ends of shoots.

Very uneven ripening of the fruits with odd shapes and reddish appearance could be Red-berry disease / Blackberry mite when a gall mite Eriophyes / Aceria essigi attacks blackberries, it overwinters under scales on the shoots and moves to eat flowers and fruit which then stay red without maturing properly. Blackberry stems are galled by hymenopteran gall-wasp Diastrophus rubi / Andricus hartigi, this mostly on outside of bush, swollen stems form with less prickles, start green go yellow then pink and purple and old ones become woody and brown, can be large specimens several inches long with hundreds of larvae. Also moves to raspberry.

Prosopis bees make small tunnels in bramble stems and frequent the flowers.
 Osmia bees do similar especially O. leucomelana.
Loganberry is bothered by Cane Spot / Anthracnose Elsinoe vneta which also bothers raspberries, purple spots with white centres on stems, leaves and flower stalks, causes fruit to be small if set at all, generally causes stunting if spots turn to cankers.
Blackberries and loganberries particularly affected by Rubus Stunt virus spread by Leaf Hoppers Aphrodes and Euscelis spp. (These do no other noticeable harm so often not noticed). The leaves distort without mosaic mottling and the stems proliferate as with a witches broom and remain stunted from the viral disease also known as Reversion / Dwarfing.

○ **Rubus idaeus, RASPBERRY**

More woodland plants needing rich moist soil, chlorotic leaves with interveinal patterning are probably from too much lime in too dry a soil.
Thought to encourage blight damage to potatoes.
Underplant with tansy, garlic and marigolds of any low growing variety.
Old references to underplanting with strawberries refer to our native wild strawberry not the modern hybrids
Birds are the most associated co-life!
Wasps also damage the fruits leaving them sucked dry.

Aphids of two varieties, pale green Rubus aphids Amphorophora rubi, and small greyish green Raspberry aphids Aphis idaei which spread the dreaded Mosaic virus and may also casue leaf curling first.

The infamous raspberry maggot is the grub of the brownish yellow Raspberry beetle Byturus tomentosus and not as often called, a weevil. The overwintering adults lay eggs in the flowers which are then consumed, and the fruits end up with scabby parts and little white grubs.

If there's a lot of damage to leaves with tiny holes, and more on the stems and shoots causing them to wilt or break then it could be the Red Legged Weevil Otiorhynchus clavipes, black with red legs, the damage starts in early spring, and will move onto currants and plums. Similar damage can be by the Clay-colured weevil Otiorhynchus singularis, another night feeder like the Red-legged weevil, these hide in debris during the day. The Clay-coloured is more destructive of the two as it strips bark, shoots as well as leaves, damage appears early summer, it overwinters as the larvae and adult in the ground where the larvae eat roots.

Strawberry Blossom weevils Anthonomus rubi often attack raspberries and lays eggs in the flowerbuds, destroyed by the feeding larvae then the whole fruit and stalk wither, this looks identical with damage by the Strawberry rhyncites Caennorhinus germaicus, both thin the crop so in the end we pick fewer but better berries.

Redberry gall mites Aceria essigi are more often found on blackberries and causes poorly ripened berries, it overwinters under scales on the shoots and moves to flowers and fruit which then stay red without maturing.

Little pink grubs in cracks in the bark on the canes are Raspberry Cane midges Thomasiniana theobaldi and these often let in disease such as Cane Blight Leptosphaeria coniophyrium, they over-winter in the soil underneath and emerge in early summer when the adults lay their eggs.

Sustains 18 Lepidoptera larva.

<u>Sole sustainer</u> Small Fanfoot Zanclognatha grisealis / nemoralis.

<u>One of three sustainers of 2</u>: Fanfoot Zanclognatha tarsipennalis others being Hedera and Salix caprea, and Sharp-angled Carpet Euphyia unangulata others being Alsine and Stellaria.

Also sustains: Pale Oak Beauty Boarmia punctinalis / consortaria, Silver Washed Fritillary Argynnis paphia, Grizzled Skipper Pyrgus malvae / alveolus, Buff Arches Habrosyne pyritoides / derasa, Emperor Saturnia pavonia / carpini, Kent Black-Arches Nola albula / albulalis, Beautiful Arches Eumichtus satura, Scarce Dagger Apatele auricoma, Saxon Hyppa rectilinear, Beautiful Carpet Mesoleuca albicillata, Common Pug Eupithecia vulgata, and Early Thorn Selenia bilunaria / illunaria.

Suffers: Raspberry Cane / Crown Borer Bembecia hylaeiformi, eggs are laid in summer, the larva overwinters at the base enters a cane, lives inside restricting growth and causing die back, after up to several years it pupates then emerges as a clearwing moth about an inch long with four yellow bands on its abdomen so looks like a wasp.

And also suffer: Raspberry moth Lampronia rubiella, reddish grub also tunnels and causes withered wilted shoots in spring, may also damage the plug of the fruit, hibernates in debris.

Plus: caterpillars that bother apples, see Malus, may also visit raspberries: Vapourer moth, the Tortrix moth, and Bud moth.

Verticillium wilt V. dahliae in Dahlias is thought to be cause of Blue Stripe in raspberries where it causes blue stripes on the cane from the base up with leaves dying on the discoloured side, or the whole cane dies if girdled, often overwinters as spores in soil so roots and stem base most often attacked. Cane Blight Leptosphaeria coniophyrium fungus, often let in by Cane midge damage, simply kills canes off.

Raspberry Spur blight Didymella applanata fungus starts at nodes and causes purple patches, these may cover the whole cane, buds at the nodes die off and spores are released from whitish patches.

Raspberry Cane spot or Anthracnose Elsinoe veneta causes purple spots with whitish centres on stems, leaves and stalks which sink into cankers or go grey with black dots. These split open cause the leaves to drop, shoots to die and fruits to distort and malform, ripen unevenly and plants do poorly. It overwinters on the old canes, also common on loganberries and other hybrids.

Raspberry Mildew Spaerotheca humili is found in crowded plantations in shade, it makes large white powdery patches on leaves and may sometimes move onto fruits.

Any plants especially old ones are prone to low vigour and yellow mottling from Raspberry Mosaic virus disease.

Raspberry Stunt virus causes the same low vigour without the mottling with numerous spindly dwarf shoots, spread by leaf-hoppers Aphrodes and Euscelis spp. (These do no other noticeable harm so often not noticed).

Avoid growing tomatoes nearby as they share a common virus Tomato Black Ring.

Raspberry Ringspot / Leaf Curl virus is spread by Longidorus nematode eelworms and spreads to redcurrants and strawberries, the leaf curling symptom of Ringspot destroyed Lloyd George, Malling Jewel, Malling Enterprise, and Norfolk Giant.

Arabis Mosaic Yellow Dwarf is also spread by nematode eelworms especially Xiphenema and also invades blackcurrants.

Symptoms of dwarfing and stunting could be pollen borne Chlorotic Leaf Spot virus.

o Salvia officinalis, SAGE

Said to protect Brassicas from many pests and aids them and carrots, inhibits cucumbers but gets on well with rosemary and dislikes rue.

Leaf-hoppers Erythroneura pallidifrons, pale yellow or white, eighth inch long, active insects may do some damage causing bleached areas on leaves, also spread to Calceolarias, Fushias, Primulas, and Verbenas.

Attacked by Eelworm nematodes causing brown spots and blackened areas, which also attacks ferns, Begonias, Coleus, Gloxinias and orchids.

Sustains: Grey Chi moth Antitype chi, and Bordered Straw Heliothis peltigera (eats mostly flowers and seeds).

o Scorzonera hispanica

Edible crop similar to salsify with long thin carrot like roots.

Attractive flowers beneficial to insects.

It may repel carrot root-fly.

Seldom suffers diseases save White Blister, Cystopus cubicus, which causes small whitish blisters on leaves, seldom serious.

- ## Secale cereale, RYE

Makes excellent ground cover for winter use producing great bulk by most springs.

Helped by a few cornflowers and helps pansies to germinate.

Hinders poppies and exudates especially of decaying residues inhibit oats and wild oats, barnyard grass and proso millet, it will choke out couch grass but also inhibits French beans, cucumbers, broad leaved weeds, maize, goosefoot and Amaranthus. Hinders germination in cress and lettuce.

Rye green manure dug in before another crop may reduce infestations of nematodes.

Sustains: White-line Dart Euoxa tritici / aquiline (young plants), Rosy Minor Procus literosa (in stems), and Brighton Wainscot Oria musculosa (in stems).

- ## Setaria italica, GERMAN MILLET

Growth inhibited by Asian weeds Bothriochloa pertusa and Dicanthium annulatum and especially by Datura inoxia. Eragrostis poaeoides, another Asian weed, exudates inhibit its germination.

- **SEX**

This is needed by most plants to produce viable seed with pollen acting as male part to fertilise the seeds. Some plants are self fertile, most are not, some are dioecious with their male and female parts on separate plants. For pollination most must have not just another of the same species but one of the right sex flowering at the same time. Common dioecious plants are; Asparagus, kiwi vines, some ancient varieties of grapevine, butcher's broom, campion, holly, Pernettya, sea buckthorn, Skimmia and some willows.

- **Sinapsis alba, WHITE MUSTARD**

Growth and germination inhibited by crimson clover and hairy vetch.
The seeds are awakened from dormancy by the presence of oat plants.
This carries most of the co-lives of Brassicas but thus also the predators that control them. Host in particular of Turnip Flea Beetle or Fly, Phyllotreta / Haltica nemorum, this makes so many holes in leaves that it can kill smaller plants and seedlings
and sadly of course Brassica Clubroot Plasmodiphora Brassicae and another fungal problem Peronospora parasitica.

- **Solanum melongena, EGGPLANT /**

AUBERGINE

Related to tomatoes, potatoes and peppers this is often grown with the last as these like the same warm rich conditions but the aubergines should be kept away from the first pair. Does well with peas, tarragon and thyme.

Digera alternifolia, an Asian weed, markedly decreases its germination.

Can be hidden from Colorado beetles (currently in USA) by interplanting with beans.

o Solanum tuberosum, POTATOES

Being highly bred and much grown these are very prey to pests and disease, keep them well away from their relations tomatoes which do not get on with cabbages while potatoes do.

Dried potato contains 4% ashes.

Potato juice made by cold extraction from the tubers, especially after the tubers have sprouted, is extremely toxic to bacteria, yet breaks down quickly in light or with heat.

Being highly bred and much grown these are very prey to pests and disease, keep them well away from their relations tomatoes.

Onions and other Alliums going before in rotation will prevent Rhizoctonia infections.

Raspberries are not good with or near potatoes as suspected of promoting blight AND the raspberries share a Ring spot virus with tomatoes so are doubly suspect.

The bird-dropping-like slug of the Lily beetle Lilloceris lilli, a bright reddy orange rather smart looking beastie, destroys the leaves also eats lilies, lily of the valley, hollyhocks, Hostas, Solomon's seal and tobacco.

In the USA aubergine plants can be used amongst potatoes as sacrificial crops to their devastating Colorado beetle Leptinotarsa / Doryphora decemlineata, a yellow and black striped ladybird like beetle with reddish orange grubs with small legs. Overwinters as adult, which eats young potato foliage, lays up to four hundred eggs in batches of two dozen on the underside of leaves, these hatch into the grubs which eat even more foliage and having two or more generations soon reach plague proportions.

This last co-life and several potato eelworms are harboured by black and woody nightshade so these should be kept weeded out, especially as they may be spurred into germination by potatoes.

Potato nematode eelworms Heterodera rostochiensis are microscopic, survive as cysts in soil for years, activated by root exudates they invade the potato destroying vigour, stunting the plant which yellows, new cysts form on roots which can just be seen by naked eye. Incorporating fresh compost and growing Tagetes whose exudates reduce populations of eelworm nematodes helps, as can green manures of mustard, barley or oats grown and dug in beforehand. For a possible way to eliminate Potato cyst nematode, see **S.** sisymbrifolium above. Horseradish is a vigorous weed planted in China to aid and protect potatoes but must be carefully removed after. Peas help potatoes considerably. Onions and other Alliums going before in rotation will prevent Rhizoctonia infections. Tagetes marigolds are beneficial as are celery, flax, Cannabis, Lamium, nasturtium and summer savoury. Potatoes are mutually beneficial with beans and maize. Sunflowers, Cucurbits, orache, many trees and raspberries are not good with or near potatoes and thought to encourage blight, and the raspberries share Ring spot virus with tomatoes so are doubly suspect.

The Green Capsid bug Lygus pabulinus is commonly found on potatoes as it has so many other common host plants, the adults are only a fifth of an inch long, green with long legs, these and their similar but smaller nymph larvae suck sap causing leaf crinkling and a loss of vigour in extreme infestations, later when the causers have left this damage may be confused with several diseases.

Spreading virus diseases are green aphid Myzus persicae and Potato aphid Macrosiphon solani which also steal sap and reduce vigour.

Occassionally potatoes are attacked by Anthomyia tuberosa root flies particularly when following poorly rotated cabbage family crops.

Sustains Death's-head Hawkmoth Acherontia atropos.

Suffers serious damage to roots from Small / Garden Swift Moth Hepialus lupulinus, this also attacks beans, parsnip, lettuce, celery, strawberry and grass roots.

The tubers may develop faults predominantly caused by incorrect growing or storing conditions ie. Tuber Blackening is caused by unbalanced feeding.

Black Heart in tubers is mostly caused by poor anaerobic storage.

Erratic watering, insufficient humus in the soil and initial pest damage can encourage self explanatory Hollow Heart, Jelly End rot, Cracking and Secondary growths (small tubers on bigger tubers).

Sudden heat waves cause Sunstroke / Heat canker.

And poor storage conditions causes Soft tubers and Premature Sprouting.

Common Potato scab Streptomyces / Actinomyces scabies causes raised rough patches on tubers, often only if weather is dry when flowers seen and small tubers forming, scabby patches just affect appearance not food value, made much worse by excess lime in soil. Scab can be reduced by mixing grass clippings, oak and or comfrey leaves in with the soil about the sets, and also by digging in a green manure of soya beans beforehand.

Corky or Powdery scab Spongospora subterranea is similar, causes more distortion and some wartiness, rare in UK, most commonly found where rotation not practised.

Tubers are attacked in store by similar looking fungus disease Dry Rot, Fusarium caeruleum where end of tubers become mummified.

Black Speck / Scurf / Collar rot, Corticium solani, may be seen as white incrustation on base of stem, can cause haulms to die, causes black scurf on skins of tubers, these are sclerotia, mostly cause poor appearance and tubers still edible.

Skin Spots Oospora pustulans are tiny pimples, turn darker if wetted, mostly superficial damage, tubers still edible but do not replant.

Silver Scurf Spondylocladium atrovirens are tiny black specks with a silvery sheen most easily seen on greening tubers while chitting, may kill eyes and so do not replant affected tubers.

Sclerotinia Rot / Stalk Break / Sclerotinia sclerotiorum, more common in wetter cooler districts where often more of a problem on carrots, other root crops and artichokes, white patches on stems, tops die or rot, sclerotia up to the size of peas formed on and in stems, these remain in soil so affected plants must be pulled and burnt.

Wart disease / Black scab / Potato Cancer / Synchytrium / Synchitrium endobioticum / Chrysophlyctis endobiotica / Oedomyces leproides is a serious and notifiable fungal disease, over-wintering sporangium of golden yellow release zoo-spores which get into potato tubers especially through the eyes, the shoots wrinkle and brown, the galled tuber develops huge cauliflower like warts, most modern varieties are resistant if not immune, no cure, burn everything, never use 'suspicious source' seed potatoes!

Potato Late Blight Phytophthora infestans first attacks leaves with blotches, then streaks run down stems, everything rots, infected tubers redden under skin, some varieties partly resistant. If you cut off tops as soon as see first infection then tubers may be saved. Also attacks tomato plants so keep separate.

Violet Root Rot, Helicobasidium purpureum / Rhizoctonia crocorum, web of loose violet / purplish threads on surface of tubers, also affects other root crops especially carrots, turnips, seakale, asparagus, no cure, burn all parts.

Pink Rot, Phytophthora erythroseptica, rare fungal disease causing pink colouration of tubers which when cut turns to purplish black, burn all parts.

Blackleg, Bacterium phytophthorum, carried in on tubers, base of stem rots and tops die, infects new tubers so do not replant, infested tuber may rot to slime and infect good tubers in store especially if damp.

Leaf-Drop Streak, small brown patches on leaves getting bigger, leaves wither and hang on not dropping off, do not replant tubers.

Many viruses trouble potatoes, mostly spread by green Peach aphid Myzus persicae and also by Potato aphid Macrosiphon solani. However our habit of saving tubers then perpetuates the problem.

Potato Leaf Roll / Leaf Curl virus disease, affected leaves curl upwards, are not limp as with most diseases but thick and crisp and may even rattle, infection reduces size of both crop and tubers.

Potato Mosaic Y virus has more deleterious effects than Leaf Roll as the leaves mottle and the plant becomes weak and stunted.

Crinkle virus is similar to Leaf Roll without the roll, the leaves thicken, pucker and crinkle.

Aucuba virus causes mottling of leaves from faint to strongly yellowed spots or patches.

- ○ **Sorghum bicolor / vulgare, SORGHUM**

Similar to maize, hindered by tomatoes, crop yield is reduced if following alfalfa or itself, also reduces growth of many grasses and weeds but may help cucumbers. The grain producing variety of sorghum inhibits wheat and sesame plants and it's own growth inhibited by Celosia argentea an Asian weed. Urgenia indica a perennial Indian weed reduces germination and growth. Purple nutsedge inhibits growth. Digera alternifolia, another Asian weed, markedly decreases germination.

- ○ **Spinacia oleracea, SPINACH**

Round seeded spinaches do best in summer but for winter and early spring sow prickly seeded spinaches.
Spinach aids humus formation being rich in saponins.
Grows well in presence of strawberries and can be used as a green manure with benefit to almost all crops except cauliflower.
It may be mutually suppressive with radishes, probably more so when either is bolting. Follows broad beans well. Can be used as a green manure with benefit to almost all crops except cauliflower. It should be much more widely used as so easily killed and incorporated. It aids humus formation being rich in saponins.

Round seeded spinaches do best in summer but for winter and early spring sow prickly seeded spinaches.

Spinach may get attacked by the Mangold fly which also attacks beetroot.

If the leaves have yellow spots and a violet or grey mould it's Downy Mildew Peronospora farinosa / effusa which causes younger leaves to thicken with spots and a greyish mat on the underside, they then yellow, brown and blacken with loss of growth, this is spread both on the seed and from debris and litter and favoured by damp conditions.

Virus Yellows is spread by the aphids Myzus persicae and Aphis fabae, the leaves develop patches of yellow turning orangey red, these mostly on the edge of leaves, these then become brittle and break up on handling, the growth is poor so are resultant crops.

Can be infected by virus Broad Bean Wilt; yellow mosaic and distortion which spreads to lettuce, pea, broad bean and other Legumes.

May also become infected by Clover Yellow Vein virus; yellow mosaic, necrosis and wilting which infects most Legumes: Cajanus, Canavalia, Cassia, Cicer, Crotolaria, Dolichos, Glycine, Hedysarum, Lathyrus, Lens, Lupinus, Medicago, Melilotus, Phaseolus, Trifolium, Trigonella, Vicia, and Vigna, and also Antirrhinum, Atriplex, Chenopodium, Coriandrum, Cucurbita, Gladiolus, Gomphrena, Nicotiana, Nicandra, Papaver, Petunia, Proboscidea, Rubus, Tetragonia, and Viola.

o **Tetragonia, NEW ZEALAND SPINACH**

May become infected by Clover Yellow Vein virus; yellow mosaic, necrosis and wilting which infects most Legumes: Cajanus, Canavalia, Cassia, Cicer, Crotolaria, Dolichos, Glycine, Hedysarum, Lathyrus, Lens, Lupinus, Medicago, Melilotus, Phaseolus, Trifolium, Trigonella, Vicia and Vigna, and also Antirrhinum, Atriplex, Chenopodium, Coriandrum, Cucurbita, Gladiolus, Gomphrena, Nicotiana, Nicandra, Papaver, Petunia, Proboscidea, Rubus, Spinacia and Viola.

o **Thymus, THYMES**

Very short lived perennial shrubby herbs with seldom grown but excellent varieties such as caraway scented Herba barona and golden Anderson's gold. Very good in the kitchen thyme is also wonderful for bees as so rich in nectar.

Exudates from thyme significantly reduce infestations of clubroot fungus of Brassicas and extracted oil controls Botrytis, Grey mould.

Thyme teas have been used to deter cabbage loopers, cabbage worms and whiteflies.

Terminal leaves are attacked by acarine gall-mites Eriophyes thomasi / Phytoptus which appear as tufts of cotton wool or mould as the leaves become clustered in filzgalls, gobular masses a third of an inch or so across covered in white hairs.

Sustains 12 Lepidoptera.

Sole sustainer of 2: Thyme Pug Eupithecia distinctaria / constrictata (eats flowers and seeds), and Large Blue Maculinea arion- which interestingly after their last moult may eat the larvae of Myrmica scabrinodis or M. laevinodis ants.

One of two sustainers of 2: Lace Border Scopula ornata / paludata other being Oreganum, and Pinion-streaked Snout Schranckia costaestrigalis other being Mentha.

One of three sustainers Light Feathered Rustic Agrotis cinerea others being Rumex species and Taraxacum.

Also sustains: Dotted-Border Wave Sterrha sylvestraria / straminata, Ashworth's Rustic Amathes ashworthii, Sussex Emerald Thalera fimbrialis, Lewes Wave Scopula immorata, Annulet Gnophos obscurata / pullata, Straw Belle Aspitates gilvaria, and V Pug Chloroclystis coronata (eats flowers).

o **Tragopogon porrifolius, SALSIFY**

A long thin carrot like vegetable similar to carrots and used to discourage carrot root-fly.

Attractive flowers beneficial to insects.

May grow well with watermelons and mustard.

May get White Blister, Cystopus cubicus, which causes small whitish blisters on leaves, seldom serious.

Rust, Puccinia hysterium, causes orange to brown spots on leaves, seldom serious but best burn all affected plants.

Very occasionally may get Powdery mildew but seldom badly unless growing conditions are poor.

o **Trifoliums, CLOVERS & TREFOILS**

Leguminous low growing plants that attract many insects especially bees, and red clover also attracts many butterflies.

One of the best short term ground covers and green manures if you can dig it in or kill it in situ with light excluding mulch.

A mixture of red clover and alsike is more effective than either alone at improving yields of hay. Clovers in turf are helped by cutting higher, closer cropping encourages first daisies then mosses instead.

Clovers are poisoned by buttercups but those can be discouraged by regular liming.

Clovers are suppressed by dressings of finely ground maize meal.

Clovers dislike henbane and may stimulate deadly nightshade.

Clovers provide cover to ground beetles, are hosts to predators of Woolly Aphis and help deter Cabbage Root Fly if sown underneath.

Sustain 8 Lepidoptera larva on most species. Interestingly Burnet moth caterpillars seek Birdsfoot trefoil plants with higher cyanide levels as this then protects them.

One of three sustainers Bordered Grey Selidosema plumaria / ericetaria others being Calluna vulgaris and Sarothamnus.

Also sustains: Belted Beauty Nyssia zonaria, Lesser Yellow Underwing Triphaena comes / orbona, Hebrew Character Orthosia gothica, Beaded Chestnut Agrochola lychnidis / pistacina, Common Emerald Hemithea aestivaria / strigata / thymiaria (before hibernation), and Black-veined Moth Siona lineata / dealbata.

Roots colonised by Rhizobium / Bacillus radicicola Leguminous partner.

After some years land may get 'Clover sick' the plants being weakened by Clover Rot Sclerotinia trifoliorum and/or Stem Eelworm Tylenchus devastatrix. This last has alternate host of oats and especially of the old tulip-rooted oats, never follow or precede these with clovers.

Can suffer fungal Violet root rot / Copper-web Helicobasidium purpureum which also attacks asparagus, beet, carrot, parsnip, potatoes and even alfalfa, also harboured by several weeds.

Clovers are main alternate host for Clover Yellow Vein virus; yellow mosaic, necrosis and wilting which spreads amongst most other Legumes: Cajanus, Canavalia, Cassia, Cicer, Crotolaria, Dolichos, Glycine, Hedysarum, Lathyrus, Lens, Lupinus, Medicago, Melilotus, Phaseolus, Trigonella, Vicia, and Vigna, and also Antirrhinum, Atriplex, Chenopodium, Coriandrum, Gladiolus, Gomphrena, Nicotiana, Nicandra, Papaver, Petunia, Proboscidea, Rubus, Spinacia, Tetragonia, Viola and some Cucurbits especially squash.

Thrips tabaci and Frankliniella occidentalis spread Tobacco Streak virus (aka Bean Red Node); red nodes, necrosis and red spots, also seed borne this also affects alfalfa, chickpea, fenugreek, Datura, soybean, Nicotiana, beans and many other plants.

- ○ **Trifolium alexandrinum, BERSEEM CLOVER**

Exudates inhibit germination of onion, carrot and tomato.

- ○ **Trifolium campestre, HOP-TREFOIL**

Sustain in addition to 8 Lepidoptera larva found on most species: Scarce Black Arches Celama aerugula / centonalis (eats flowers and leaves), and Bordered Straw Heliothis peltigera (mostly on flowers and seeds).

- Trifolium dubium, LESSER YELLOW TREFOIL

Sustains in addition to 8 Lepidoptera larva found on most species: Silver Cloud Xylomiges conspicullaris, and Bordered Straw Heliothis peltigera (mostly on flowers and seeds).

- Trifolium hybridum, ALSIKE CLOVER

Inhibited from germinating by exudates of white clover.

- Trifolium incarnatum, CRIMSON CLOVER

Annual especially useful as green manure and as generally beneficial companion.
Exudates inhibit germination and growth of onion, carrot and tomato, maize, cotton, Italian ryegrass and wild mustard.

- Trifolium pratense, RED / PURPLE CLOVER

Foliage contains from 6-11% mineral ash.
Red clover is preferred host to Dodder and Broom-rape parasitic plants.

Inhibited by exudates of white clover, also Erica australis inhibits its germination.

Root extracts inhibit germination and seedling growth of wheat.

Once known as Bee Bread as particularly good for humble and bumble bees.

May be parasitised by Dodder and Broom-rape.

Attacked by Clover 'Pear-shaped' / Purple Clover Weevils Apion apricans / flavifemoratum which feed on seeds turning blossoms rusty and withering flowerheads.

Flowers are particularly rich in nectar.

Sustains 13 Lepidoptera larva in addition to 8 Lepidoptera larva found on most species: Grass Eggar Lasiocampa trifolii, Pearly Underwing Peridroma porphyrea / saucia, Common Blue Polyommatus icarus / alexis, Mazarine Blue Cyaniris semiargus / acis, Pale Clouded Yellow Colias hyale, Clouded Yellow Colias croceus / edusa, Mother Shipton Euclidimera mi, Burnet Companion Eetypa glyphica, Scarce Black Arches Celama aerugula / centonalis (eats flowers and leaves), Marbled Clover Heliothis dipsacea / viriplaca (eats flowers and seeds), Chalk Carpet Ortholitha bipunctaria, and Bloxworth Blue Everes argiades / tiresias (eats flowers and leaves).

Suffers Garden Dart Euoxa nigricans.

- **Trifolium repens, WHITE / DUTCH CLOVER**

Contains over 9% ash with lime 3% and phosphoric acid 0.6%.

Exudates inhibit its own germination and that of many Legumes and grasses especially alsike clover, red clover, lotus, cocksfoot and perennial ryegrass. Erica australis, inhibits its germination. Eupatorium adenophorum and E. riparium, reduces germination. Stevia eupatoria seriously reduces germination and growth.

This is the one for honeybees as the flower suits their short tongues.

Flowers galled by acarine gall- mites, this may cause phyllody where floral parts become leafy.

Leaflets galled by Dipteron gall-midge, Dasyneura / Cecidomyia trifolii which rolls them up to form a pod of yellow to reddy brown.

Sustains 14 Lepidoptera in addition to 8 Lepidoptera larva found on most species: Heart & Club Agrotis clavis / corticea, Common Blue Polyommatus icarus / alexis, Mazarine Blue Cyaniris semiargus / acis, Pale Clouded Yellow Colias hyale, Clouded Yellow Colias croceus / edusa, Mother Shipton Euclidimera mi, Burnet Companion Eetypa glyphica, Shaded Broad-Bar Ortholitha chenopodiata / limitata / mensuraria, Chalk Carpet Ortholitha bipunctaria, Latticed Heath Chiasma clathrata, Scarce Black Arches Celama aerugula / centonalis (eats flowers and leaves), Bloxworth Blue Everes argiades / tiresias (eats flowers and leaves), and Hoary Footman Eilema caniola (algae and lichens).

Suffers Garden Dart Euoxa nigricans.

May become infected by Clover Yellow Vein virus; yellow mosaic, necrosis and wilting which infects most other Legumes and also Antirrhinum, Atriplex, Chenopodium, Coriandrum, Cucurbita, Gladiolus, Gomphrena, Nicotiana, Nicandra, Papaver, Petunia, Proboscidea, Rubus, Spinacia, Tetragonia and Viola.

- o **Trifolium subterraneum, SUBTERRANEAN / BURROWING CLOVER**

Chokes out weeds well, even competing with bracken.

- o **Trigonella foenum-graecum,**

FENUGREEK

Legume, the seed is the spice, as with garlic fenugreek can be smelt in the perspiration of those eating much of it.

May become infected by Clover Yellow Vein virus; yellow mosaic, necrosis and wilting which infects most other Legumes: Cajanus, Canavalia, Cassia, Cicer, Crotolaria, Dolichos, Glycine, Hedysarum, Lathyrus, Lens, Lupinus, Medicago, Melilotus, Phaseolus, Trifolium, Vicia and Vigna, and also Antirrhinum, Atriplex, Chenopodium, Coriandrum, Cucurbita, Gladiolus, Gomphrena, Nicotiana, Nicandra, Papaver, Petunia, Proboscidea, Rubus, Spinacia, Tetragonia and Viola.

o **Triticum aestivum / turgidum / vulgare, WHEAT**

Reduces to 2.4% ashes which contain 22% potash, 16% soda, 2% lime, 10% magnesia, 1.4% iron oxide, negligible manganese oxide, 49% phosphoric acid, 0.2% sulphuric acid, little silica and little chlorine. Mixed cropping of wheat with field beans can give 30% higher yield with 20% increase in net value. Crop yields helped by small amounts of chamomile, corn cockle, mustard or maize. White mustard under sown at 12 kg/Ha improve yields as do vetches.

Hindered by lentils, poppies, violets, bindweed, tulips, cherry, dogwood and pine trees, wild oats, Argemone Mexicana, Chenopodium album and C. murale, Cassia sophera and Crotolaria pallida, Phalaris minor, Eupatorium adenophorum, E. riparium, Anaphalis araneosa, Galinsoga ciliata, Parthenium hysterophorus, Proboscidea louisianica, Salvia syriaca, Sasa cernua, all of which may inhibit germination and or growth. Purple nutsedge, and Saccharum spontaneum inhibit growth. Alfalafa, plantains, Ageratum conyzoides, Euphorbia geniculate, and red clover root extracts inhibit germination and seedling growth of wheat. Leaf leachate of Pluchea lanceolata an Asian weed hinders growth, Borreria articularis, another Asian weed, suppresses growth. Decaying residues of pea, broad bean, soya bean, lupin, chickpea, safflower, sunflower, rape, sorghum, barley, oats and wheat itself all inhibit root growth of wheat. Couch grass blocks phosphate uptake by the wheat so should be eliminated.

Wheat inhibits broad leaved weeds especially fat hen. Wheat straw residues hinder cotton and barley growth.

The flower of wheat is galled by a nematode eelworm Tylenchus tritici / scandens causing 'corn cockle', 'purples', 'false ergot', 'peppercorn gall' when the ovary fails to set seeds but swells and turns purple to brown or black, this falls to release up to fifteen thousand new nematodes, these may survive twenty years, and worse, the nematodes carry a fungus Dilophospora alopecuri which causes 'Twist disease'.

Sustains 6 Lepidoptera larva.

<u>Sole sustainer of</u> Rustic Shoulder-Knot Apamea sordens / basilinea (seeds, possibly of other grasses).

<u>One of three sustainers</u> Flounced Rustic Luperina testacea (roots) others being Avena and Hordeum.

Also sustains: Rosy Minor Procus literosa (in stems), Pale Mottled Yellow Caradrina clavipalpis / cubicularis / quadripunctata (seeds), Rosy Rustic Hydraecia micacea (in stems), and Brighton Wainscot Oria musculosa (in stem).

Berberis, especially the wild form over-winters rust and should be kept well away from wheat as berberis is galled by 'Black rust of wheat' fungi Puccinia graminis forming yellow brown spots and orange cluster-cups underneath the leaves, after infesting the wheaty this rust lies dormant through winter then erupts basidospores which reinfest the berberis.

- ○ **Vaccinium**

Our native Bilberry, V. myrtillus and Cranberry, V. oxycoccus have recently been superceded in the garden by the more productive American versions of Blueberry, V. corymbosum hybrids and Cranberry, V. macrocarpon, these may well soon exhibit similar co-lives as the natives.

Lime haters. Most have edible berries.

Certainly Blueberries are subject to Scale insects. Russula paludosa with a rose or strawberry coloured to orangey yellow cap is considered edible, it prefers damp pine or spruce forests, peat bogs and the company of bilberries.

Cortinarius / Dermocybe cinnamomeoluteus is edible but risky as hard to tell from poisonous species, has a yellowish brownish olive cap with radial markings, gills start yellow going to brown and the yellow stipe has little fibrils spread over it, the yellowish flesh smells of beetroot, this is also very common in coniferous forests on acid soil.

- ○ **Valerianella, CORN SALAD**

Edible crop, will grow in winter making useful green manure /fodder for hens.

Sustains Rosy Wave moth Scopula emutaria.

Vicia, BROAD / FAVA / FIELD BEANS and VETCHES

Accumulate Cobalt, Copper, Nitrogen, Phosphorous and Potassium.

Will germinate even in winter months.

These are Legumes so enrich the soil.

Beans may be grown with cereals as mixed feed for animals when both crops benefit from pest and disease protection producing more in total fodder than either alone. Once used for food but now more for fodder, and as cover and green manure crops. They grow well with oats and rye benefiting them if not in too great a quantity.

Field crops of small beans known as Tick or Horse beans, smell sweet and provide a lot of nectar for bees, the haulm makes a good base for bedding and sheet composts. Tick beans are heavy croppers with typically a ton and a half per acre giving eight hundred or so pounds of protein and nearly a ton and a half of carbohydrate but little oil with only forty pounds or so per acre. Beans may be grown with cereals as mixed feed for animals when both crops benefit from pest and disease protection producing more in total fodder than either alone Many have gland stipules at base of leaves.

Aphids on vetches are preferred food of some ladybirds enabling them to multiply.

Sustains: Grass Eggar Lasiocampa trifolii, and Shaded Broad-Bar Ortholitha chenopodiata / limitata / mens uraria.

May be infected by Clover Yellow Vein virus; yellow mosaic, necrosis and wilting which infects most other Legumes: Cajanus, Canavalia, Cassia, Cicer, Crotolaria, Dolichos, Glycine, Hedysarum, Lathyrus, Lens, Lupinus, Medicago, Melilotus, Phaseolus, Trifolium, Trigonella, Vigna, and also Antirrhinum, Atriplex, Chenopodium, Coriandrum, Cucurbita, Gladiolus, Gomphrena, Nicotiana, Nicandra, Papaver, Petunia, Proboscidea, Rubus, Spinacia, Tetragonia and Viola.

Also infected by Bean Curly Dwarf mosaic; mosaic, stunting and rugosity, also infects Phaseolus species, soybean, pea, chickpea, lentil, mung bean and Leguminous weeds,

- ○ **Vicia cracca, TUFTED VETCH**

Bombus terrestris bites hole in side of flower to steal nectar.

One of three sustainers Black-neck Lygephila pastinum others being Astragalus glycphyllos and Vicia cracca.

Also sustains: Scarce Black-neck Lygephila craccae, Wood White Leptidea sinapis, and Sub-angled Wave Scopula nigropunctata / strigilaria.

○ Vicia faba, BROAD BEANS

Ashes contain 21% potash, 19% soda, 7% lime, 9% magnesia, 1% iron oxide, negligible manganese oxide, 38% phosphoric acid, 13% sulphuric acid, 3% silica and 1.5% chlorine.

Mutually beneficial with potatoes both can be sown in the autumn for earlier crops if the winter is mild. The seedling beans protect the early potato shoots from wind and frost. Broad beans are a good crop to follow with maize as they leave a rich moist soil and stump stubs give wind protection to the young shoots.

The flowers are often cut into by buff-tailed and small earth humble bees whose tongues are too short to reach the nectar by legitimate means, this results in reduced pollination of the seeds and many flowers produce pods with fewer seeds than the standard or just abort.

Beans are often autumn sown to avoid the Black Bean aphid aka Black Fly, Dolphin and Collier, Aphis rumicis / fabae which also attacks other beans but not as frequently, this may be discouraged by growing summer savory nearby which also cooks well with beans, nipping out the bean tips above the flowers is more effective. Black bean aphids overwinter on the wild spindle tree, furze, fat hen and black nightshade and also attack beetroot and spinach. (These aphids often killed en masse in humid warm weather by fungal disease Entomophthora spp.)

Seeds may be damaged by Bean beetle Bruchus granarius / rufimanus, the Pea beetle B. pisorum and the Broad Bean beetle Acanthoscelides obtectus all cause holes and transparent patches in the seeds, the adults lay eggs on the pods and the larvae eat into the seeds, the pupae may not be noticed in saved seed and then sown with the next crop.

Planted with gooseberries they discourage sawfly caterpillars.

Suffer Small / Garden Swift Moth Hepialus lupulinus on roots, also suffers Silver Gamma / Y moth Plusia gamma.

Chocolate Spot, Botrytis cinerea / fabae, instead of usual grey fluffy mould plants get dark chocalate coloured spots on leaves and streaks on stems and may defoliate even die, pods and seeds may also suffer, worse in wet soils and unbalanced conditions, this also attacks many other plants and overwinters on debris.

Other leaf spots caused by Acochyta fabae, Cercospora fabae etc. often just damaging to appearance rarely fatal, indeed frost damage and aphid bites may also cause similar spots to no great detriment.

Rust, Uromyces fabae, typical spotty rust fungus attack, improve conditions but in general more of a problem with appearance than growth.

Broad Bean wilt virus, yellow mosaic and distortion, spread by aphids, invades large number of crops and other plants including lettuce, pea, spinach and other Legumes.

○ Vicia sativa, COMMON VETCH

Flower and more often leaf-bud galled by Dipteron gall-midge Contarinia / Diplosis / Cecidomyia loti, flower distorted fails to open and becomes downy, yellow, pink or reddish brown. When the leaf is galled it forms a miniature bunch of bananas greenish yellow or brown. This also attacks Bush vetch below.

○ Vicia sepium, BUSH VETCH

The flowers designed to exclude smaller insects and common Humble bee Bombus terrestris bites hole through side to get at nectar.
Sustains: Scarce Black-neck Lygephila craccae, and Cream Wave Scopula floslactata / remutata / remutaria.

○ Vicia sylvatica, WOOD VETCH

Sustains Scarce Black-neck Lygephila craccae.

○ Vicia villosa, HAIRY VETCH

Inhibits germination and growth of onion, carrot and tomato, maize, cotton, Italian ryegrass and wild mustard.

○ Vigna, MUNG BEANS

Warm climate Legumes

May be infected by Bean Curly Dwarf mosaic; mosaic, stunting and rugosity, also infects Phaseolus species, soybean, pea, chickpea, lentil, broad bean, and Leguminous weeds.

Also may be infected by Clover Yellow Vein virus; yellow mosaic, necrosis and wilting which infects most other Legumes: Cajanus, Canavalia, Cassia, Cicer, Crotolaria, Dolichos, Glycine, Hedysarum, Lathyrus, Lens, Lupinus, Medicago, Melilotus, Phaseolus, Trifolium, Trigonella and Vicia, and also Antirrhinum, Atriplex, Chenopodium, Coriandrum, Cucurbita, Gladiolus, Gomphrena, Nicotiana, Nicandra, Papaver, Petunia, Proboscidea, Rubus, Spinacia, Tetragonia,and Viola.

o Vitis vinifera, GRAPEVINE

Growing vines over trees is from Classical times, most often chosen were elm, mulberry then poplar. Do not overfeed vines! Ancient instructions to bury a dead horse / sheep / cow under a vine is hardly easy or hygienic, and is foolish.

Aided by blackberries, hyssop and mustard.

Legumes should be incorporated if vines are put down to grass.

Grapes have been thought inhibited by laurels, radish and cabbages since classical times and Gerard thought they did not like horseradish.

Tomatoes give off volatile exudates that hinder vines.

Grapes most powerful associated co-life is the birds who will rob you.

Vine Weevil can weaken and kill vines.

Under cover Mealy Bug, Tortrix moths and Thrips do their worst.

In the UK we are lucky as we can grow grapes on their own roots (ie we can grow new plants from rooted cuttings) as we have no Phylloxera aphids eating them here but on the Continent and with most bought vines they are grown on resistant rootstocks. The American Vitis labrusca hybrid varieties seem naturally resistant.

Scale Lecanium persicae which also attacks peaches and nectarines is yellowish greenish brown and a quarter inch by a sixth ovals.

Soft scale Pulvinaria vitis prefers grapevines but will move onto currants, it makes a conspicuous white woolly wad in which the eggs are protected, the larvae move out and form a scale once settled. Sustains: Striped Hawkmoth Celerio livornica, Silver Striped Hawkmoth Hippotion celerio, and occasionally Elephant Hawkmoth Deilephila elpenor.

Vine Powdery mildew Uncinula necator attacks leaves and fruits and the latter split once it has hardened their skin, most often a problem in dull weather or shade, disappears in hot bright conditions.

Downy mildew Plasmopara viticola attacks only the leaves but can seriously reduce growth. Both are made worse by sudden changes in atmosphere, dryness at the roots and fluctuating humidity.

Black rot Guignardia bidwellii causes brown irregular patches on young leaves, resembles scald but black specks can be seen, then fungus moves to berries which dry up and shrivel.

Ripe Rot Glomerella cingulata causes swollen oblong patches on the fruits which exude stickiness and become purple, highly infectious.

Shanking is similar where the stem of the bunch of fruits dies turning brown and shrivelling, the fruits stop developing normally and even if near ripe tend to be bitter.

- ## Zea mays, CORN / MAIZE / SWEET CORN

Maize as grown worldwide are varieties for animal fodder and are seldom good eating whereas Sweet Corn are varieties chosen for their soft sweet kernels. Popping corn is a special variety and needs a very hot summer. Mealies are African forms of maize. Maize may produce up to fifty tons per acre with a dry matter yield of five tons containing three hundred pounds of oil and five hundred pounds of ash. Sweet corn and maize was traditionally grown in hillocks covering a dead fish. Incorporating fishmeal, seaweed meal or compost is the modern alternative as they need very rich soil.

Heavy dressings of maize flour to swards stimulates growth in the grass.

Maize uses pollen to prevent nearby plants setting viable seed; just ten grains of their pollen on the stigma of other plants can prevent them setting viable seed, especially bad for watermelons! Pollen and or leaf residues from maize hinder Amaranthus germinating.

Maize contains allelopathic compounds that check root growth in annual weeds and suppress clover and dandelions in lawns.

It's own germination is inhibited by its own residues, by exudates and run off from rye, soya beans, taro, tobacco, Amaranthus, yellow foxtail, oats, wild oats, mixed grass hay, crimson clover and hairy vetch. The weeds Xanthium strumarium and Urgenia indica reduce both germination and growth. Growth is inhibited by Asian weeds Bothriochloa pertusa and Celosia argentea. The weeds velvetleaf (Abutilon), fat hen (Chenopodium), redroot pigweed (Amaranthus) and yellow foxtail (Setaria glauca), seriously reduce growth and seed production. In the USA maize is subject to serious inhibition by Quackgrass. Tomatoes inhibit maize.

Soya bean residues once these have been well incorporated stop hindering germination and increase maize yields. Intercropping maize with sunflowers increases yields of both. Maize should follow a Legume or grow with them, it does well with all beans and the Basques grow runner beans up and over their corn. It does well with peas which allegedly crop for longer (if enough moisture is present). Their light shade makes them friendly to cucumbers, melons, squashes, courgettes, marrows and even to potatoes. Brussel's sprouts do least badly of all the Brassicas with maize and some others; Kale, savoys and broccolis, can also be inter-planted as when the sweet corn is cleared in early autumn it allows them a final spurt of growth before winter. The dried stems, leaves and all, tied in bundles and secreted in dry places such as inside evergreens and under eaves make remarkably popular homes for over-wintering ladybirds.

The Frit fly Oscinis frit can ruin maize plants, also attacks oats, the eggs laid in spring hatch to tiny legless larvae which eat into the growing point and the plant is stunted even killed, new leaves are stunted and crops suffer, there can be up to three generations in a year, then larvae overwinter in grasses.

Sustains Scarce Bordered Straw Heliothis armigera.

Smut Ustilago maydis causes large boils which ooze on any part of the plant especially the cobs, the infection is purely local with boils forming wherever spores land, it does not progress through the whole plant though yields drop because of infected cobs and any part of the plant may become distorted, commoner in warm wet years when temperature is approx. 86°F. Chlamydospores overwinter on debris and remain viable for up to five years. Oddly the infected cob is considered an esculental delicacy in some countries.

Printed in Poland
by Amazon Fulfillment
Poland Sp. z o.o., Wrocław

50231874R00146